# The Art and Science of Ballet Dancing and Teaching

This book offers an inside view of ballet as the art form we see on stages today, detailing how expressive movement is initiated and controlled, and discussing the importance of embedding creativity and expressivity within ballet technique from the dancer's first lesson to their final performance.

Janet Karin O.A.M. promotes ballet as a holistic art form resulting from the integration of mind, brain and body, and describes the motor control factors that can enhance or interfere with achievement. Throughout, professional dancers' personal experiences illuminate the text, from the euphoria of 'flow' to the search for creativity and harmony, from the debilitating effects of anxiety, trauma and pain to the reward of artistic autonomy. Teaching is presented from a philosophical viewpoint, enriching and extending the child's innate movement skills and expressive power.

Practical yet reflective, this is an essential guide for dancers as well as dance educators and students.

**Janet Karin** O.A.M. has been Principal Dancer with The Australian Ballet, then a ballet teacher, dance educator, somatic educator, writer and dance science researcher. She has served as President of the International Association for Dance Medicine & Science and has presented numerous papers at international dance science conferences. Her collaboration with five universities has resulted in thirteen published research papers. Janet is now writing freelance and mentoring doctoral students.

# The Art and Science of Ballet Dancing and Teaching
Integrating Mind, Brain and Body

Janet Karin

LONDON AND NEW YORK

Designed cover image: After the Rain © by Christopher Wheeldon. Dancers: Robyn Hendricks and Robert Curran. Photo courtesy of The Australian Ballet. Photographer: Jess Bialek

First published 2024
by Routledge
4 Park Square, Milton Park, Abingdon, Oxon OX14 4RN

and by Routledge
605 Third Avenue, New York, NY 10158

*Routledge is an imprint of the Taylor & Francis Group, an informa business*

© 2024 Janet Karin

The right of Janet Karin to be identified as author of this work has been asserted in accordance with sections 77 and 78 of the Copyright, Designs and Patents Act 1988.

All rights reserved. No part of this book may be reprinted or reproduced or utilised in any form or by any electronic, mechanical, or other means, now known or hereafter invented, including photocopying and recording, or in any information storage or retrieval system, without permission in writing from the publishers.

*Trademark notice*: Product or corporate names may be trademarks or registered trademarks, and are used only for identification and explanation without intent to infringe.

*British Library Cataloguing-in-Publication Data*
A catalogue record for this book is available from the British Library

ISBN: 978-1-032-49721-1 (hbk)
ISBN: 978-1-032-49720-4 (pbk)
ISBN: 978-1-003-39518-8 (ebk)

DOI: 10.4324/9781003395188

Typeset in Galliard
by Apex CoVantage, LLC

I dedicate this book to the memory of
my beloved daughter, Isobel.

# Contents

*Acknowledgements*   ix

Introduction: A lifetime of discovery   1

## PART 1
## Unveiling dancers' artistry   3

  1  Performing: a transcendent experience   5
  2  Breath, movement, emotion and music   11
  3  Expressivity, harmony, creativity and artistry   19
  4  Technique, training and changes in dancers' brains   30
  5  Dealing with challenges   41

## PART 2
## The magical motor system   49

  6  The science behind the scenes   51
  7  Pathways to new skills   61

## PART 3
## The art of training dancers   69

  8  Our role as ballet teachers   71
  9  Skills in cueing and feedback   77
10  Discovering technique   84

| 11 | The speaking body | 94 |
| 12 | Discovering the dancer inside | 106 |
| Afterword | | 114 |

*Glossary of ballet terms*   115
*References*   117
*Index*   124

# Acknowledgements

The hundreds of dancers I danced with, the thousands of students I taught, the many researchers I worked with and my colleagues across the world have all contributed to this book because every debate, every difference of opinion, every inspiration has contributed to my understanding of dance and dance science – and hence to the content and structure of this book.

More specifically, I acknowledge my gratitude to Carolyn Carattini D.C.I. – a true educator who advised me wisely and generously throughout the writing process. I also acknowledge the wise contribution of my advisory readers: Julia Barry MPhil, Tim Dunlop PhD, Matthew Lawrence GradCert, Sanna Nordin-Bates PhD, Michelle Potter PhD and Rachel Ward PhD. My grateful thanks also go to David Hallberg, Artistic Director of The Australian Ballet, for his warm interest in my project.

As a long-time writer but first-time book author, I thank Routledge's Lucy Batrouney and Georgia Oman, whose friendly guidance took me through the publishing process. Their support for my project is very much appreciated. I also value the tireless encouragement offered by my family and friends. I owe my enjoyment of the writing process to the generous enthusiasm of everyone involved.

Finally, I acknowledge the Australian Boon Wurrung and Wurundjeri people of the Kulin Nation and their elders, past, present and emerging, as the traditional custodians of the land on which I wrote this book.

# Introduction

## A lifetime of discovery

*In the wings, a dancer is enlivened by the music, eager to burst on stage in a flurry of energy and speed.*

*Another dancer is still and quiet, breathing slowly while forming a cocoon around herself, focusing the emotion and creativity that will illuminate her performance on stage.*

*Nearby, a dancer is jumping higher and higher, revving up the dynamic power he will need to perform their next variation.*

*Another dancer is scrolling through their mental checklist – 'Do this and that', 'Don't forget this', 'That wasn't great last time' . . .*

*One dancer is meditating in a dark corner, hoping to calm the anxiety and fear they usually experience before solo roles.*

*In another theatre, a dancer is creating their own reality. They sense the cold night air, a dark starry sky, the eerie stillness of their forest world. Soon they will glide through their mystic realm.*

I have written this book for all those who, like me, have wondered what is 'inside' the visible reality of the dancing body. How does the miracle of beautiful, expressive dancing happen? This question has mesmerised me from my earliest ballet classes. Now, after many decades as a dancer, teacher and dance science researcher, I offer my understanding of the mystery within dance to all those who share my wonder. The book is written primarily for dancers, ballet staff, ballet teachers and vocational and academic dance students, but I hope it may be of interest to parents, audience members, health practitioners and anyone else who wishes to know more about the inner workings of the dancer's mind and body.

I have lived in four different but interacting worlds: as a student, as a professional ballet dancer, as a ballet teacher and finally as a researcher in dance science. Moving from one world to the next has been a logical progression, a continuity of creativity and curiosity. As a student and as a professional dancer, I loved the physical sensation, the emotional power and aesthetics of movement, while ballet's intellectual challenges stimulated me to explore the unique nature of ballet as an art among others. What is special about ballet? Why does it have such a profound effect on dancers and audiences alike? How can a strict, one might say rigid, technique produce seemingly natural expressivity? Clearly, these apparent miracles of communication are not produced solely by training and experience.

When I began teaching, these questions became even more significant. To do full justice to my students, I needed to go much further than technical training – I needed to solve the mystery of dancing and ballet. Although I suspect a full understanding of dance will always remain somewhat elusive, dance science reveals the internal processes supporting dancers' performances and the experiential learning behind the development of their

DOI: 10.4324/9781003395188-1

artistry. Dance science has deepened my understanding while retaining, possibly increasing, the passion and power of dance performance. In this book, I hope to broaden the dance world's perspective on what a successful dancer is and does, and so make my own contribution to this much-loved artform.

Given my own background, much of the book's content may appear to explore dance from a ballet perspective. In fact, I also address themes relevant to dance in general, and to those dancing in any capacity – as professionals, as students and as amateurs. I also hope audience members may enjoy an insight into the intricate partnership between dancers' minds and bodies as they prepare and perform on stage. Throughout, I have illuminated the text with the words of successful dancers from a range of training approaches, dancing a range of repertoire in ballet companies across the world. These artists, most of whom are currently performing and a few who are now teaching, have entrusted me with intimate, honest glimpses into their dancing lives. I pay tribute to their selfless generosity towards me, and towards you, our readers.

The contributing dancers are Pol Andres Thio, Dimity Azoury, Benedicte Bemet, Havilah Blum, Carolyn Carattini, Joseph Chapman, Brett Chynoweth, Noah Dunlop, Alicia Fabry, Mia Heathcote, Matthew Lawrence, Jake Mangakahia, Kirsty Martin, David Power, Zarina Stahnke and Nancie Woods. They have gained their experience and honed their artistry while performing in Australia (The Australian Ballet, Queensland Ballet, Tasmanian Ballet, GWB Entertainment); Canada (National Ballet of Canada); France (Ballet de l'Opéra National du Rhin, Ballet Nice Méditerranée); Germany (Dart Dance Company Dresden, Frankfurter Ballet-Bühne, Semperoper Ballet); UK (Birmingham Royal Ballet, The Royal Ballet); and the USA (Ballet Chicago, Ballet Oklahoma, Carolina Ballet, Dallas Ballet, Delta Festival Ballet New Orleans, Sacramento Ballet, Saint Louis Ballet, Santa Fe Opera, Stars of American Ballet and Texas Ballet Theater). Their thoughts appear as italicised, indented paragraphs throughout the book.

The structure of this book is unusual, but intentionally so. By starting at the pinnacle of dancers' performing lives and progressing towards early ballet training, it reverses the trajectories of individual careers. This strategy places the focus of Part 1 on what a ballet dancer is and does – the experiences and processes underlying their performances and their search for honesty, creativity and artistry. However, few dancers and teachers are aware of how the body creates skilled, expressive, creative movement. Therefore, Part 2 describes the internal dance between our motor systems, our senses, our emotions and our bodies, and our capacity to improve performance. Finally, Part 3 questions how we can create a pathway from young children's naturally expressive movement to the complex physical and emotional understanding of dancers who will create the future of dance and ballet for decades to come. There is inevitably some cross-over between sections of the book because human bodies and minds are closely integrated, and concepts such as technique, emotion, learning, history and philosophical matters cannot be neatly isolated. The reader many wish to consult the glossary for descriptions of ballet terms. In addition, the index directs the reader to scientific concepts and other relevant information.

Throughout the book, readers will notice references to certain research papers, especially when the findings have been quoted. I have included them within the text (and listed them in full at the back of the book) in the hope that one or two readers might explore a few papers on their areas of interest and become engrossed in the fascinating world of dance and movement research. In essence, I am hoping my overview of ballet may offer information and inspiration for everyone involved in, or interested in, this physical expression of our human spirit – ballet.

# Part 1
# Unveiling dancers' artistry

# 1 Performing

## A transcendent experience

In dance, the human body becomes an expressive instrument, transmitting emotions, sensations and thoughts directly into the minds and bodies of individual people sitting far away, in the dark, at the back of a theatre. To begin to understand this phenomenon, the chapter explores themes raised by dancers as they describe their own performing experiences and their development as creative artists. Clearly, performing can be a transcendent experience for us as dancers.

> *I go into that space of complete submersion in the task where I feel like a powerful creature, highly aware. I use the word* creature *because I feel bigger and more connected than what my physical body seems capable of.*

We recognise that hard work and mental preparation do not guarantee a similar experience in performance, so its very elusiveness makes it even more enticing.

> *Having done all the necessary preparation rehearsing in the studio, the ability to come onstage and perform without thinking and purely feeling is the ideal that I try to reach every performance. It's what I think every memory of 'the best show I ever had' from any dancer is.*

Clearly, these experiences are far beyond normal day-to-day pleasure. They signify a state that can be described as euphoric. Indeed, it may lie at the heart of the fulfilment we seek through performance.

> *You simply fly through the entire piece without feeling like anything could go wrong. Complete and utter bliss bursting from within to the audience and everyone onstage.*

However, experiences such as these do not occur in every performance. One dancer who often achieves complete immersion regards less-rewarding performances as instructive.

> *Of course, all these concepts and experiences would fluctuate from day to day because we are human.*

Complete immersion in the act of dancing can be quite rare for some dancers, even those with successful careers.

DOI: 10.4324/9781003395188-3

> *I remember when I first went onstage as an eight-year-old, I felt as if I could do nothing but smile. I was beaming from the inside out. To dance in front of an audience invigorated me, it brought me such joy that I hadn't really felt before. Sadly, when the realities of the dance world began to hit me in my teen years, I lost hold of that feeling. Yes, I smiled onstage, but the nerves and fear of failure were often very hard to shake. I don't know if I ever got it back. Most of the time it was a mental struggle against not being enough.*

Others can be unsettled by the absence of mental oversight typical of exceptional performance.

> *I often find myself feeling euphoric and have to control a rush of adrenaline if something feels technically easy or I accomplish something particularly technically difficult with aplomb.*

The euphoria reported by many of these dancers is defined as 'flow', or 'being in the zone'. In 1990, Hungarian-American psychologist Professor Mihály Csíkszentmihályi defined 'flow' as a state of profound pleasure resulting from complete immersion in an activity (Csíkszentmihályi, 1990). The professor and later researchers described the following elements necessary for the experience of flow:

### a. A balance between challenge and skills

A task that is too challenging may lead to anxiety and fear, whereas a task that does not challenge the dancer's skill may feel boring. The most rewarding experiences occur when challenge and skill are both very high.

> *Considering the time, attention to detail and focus that dancers put into rehearsing and throughout class, to be able to have the sensation that anything you do is going to be exactly as you pictured it in your mind is something I hope that I could have every single class and show.*

However, the situation can be fluid. Inadequate rehearsal, unfamiliar conditions or injury may cause a temporary imbalance between skill and challenge. Fear and other insecurities may lead a dancer to believe their skill does not match the challenge.

> *It's very easy to lose confidence in a role, or in a particular step. Strangely, it can happen after someone praises you for the way you perform a certain movement. From then on, you can become obsessed with not meeting their expectation.*

### b. Complete concentration on the task

There can be numerous distractors during performance, from other dancers and stage crew, the orchestra, and minor glitches in tempo, lighting and staging elements. To gain flow, a dancer must focus on the essence of the role, how the movement can speak to the audience.

> *I try not to let thoughts take over the emotional and physical feeling when performing. I find that when I think less and focus more on the music and the narrative or emotion I want to portray, there is more flow in my performance.*

## c. Clear goals and immediate feedback

Although there are many elements involved in preparing for performance, dancers benefit by developing 'a strong personal sense of what they want to do' (Csíkszentmihályi, 1990). Ideally, feedback is intrinsic rather than depending on external factors such as applause or praise.

> *Not only can the performance be meaningful to you personally but also to so many people watching, and when the audience understands and is with you it creates even more momentum to become a very powerful force or, in a way, spirit in the theatre.*

## d. A deep but effortless involvement in the task

When dancers become completely absorbed in their performance, they have no mental space for extraneous matters. Their movements become spontaneous, with no sensation of effort or difficulty.

> *In some performances I knew that my sheer presence was enough. My deeper, inner instincts, my response to the music, character, other dancers and space – I knew they would all fire and flow exactly as they needed to, and all I had to do was be there. I suppose it's like being a vessel.*

## e. A sense of control

In training, dancers strive for physical and technical control – of their 'inner core', their turn-out, their balance, their line and so on. In a state of flow, 'control' is the sense that everything controls itself.

> *I can do what I want, let the things inside of me express themselves freely (without interruption or correction or being stalled in any way). In this way – even when you're performing a role or delving into something outside yourself – it always feels like a distillation of you: some essence of you is driving things.*

## f. The sense of time is fluid

A characteristic of flow is the sensation that time passes much more quickly or slowly than it does in reality. Nuyens and colleagues proposed that flow states direct most of the brain's attentional resources to the ongoing activity, resulting in fewer resources available for time perception, most often leading to an underestimation of duration (Nuyens et al., 2019). Therefore, it can feel as if a long *pas de deux* is over in a flash.

> *In the zone, time is fast and slow, at the same time.*

Even the sense of space can change.

> *The world feels bigger, as if you can soar into space, and time seems to expand so you experience the moment to its utmost.*

## g. Autotelia

An autotelic experience is a situation in which an individual values an experience as its own reward. Although it is likely all dancers hope for this situation, some are hampered by technical or emotional insecurities, injury and other factors beyond their control. On the other hand, some dancers, by nature or by intention, readily commit themselves to creating an autotelic experience.

> *I never considered myself a performer. I never liked to dance 'for' anyone, because that seemed to take me away from myself, instead of connecting to what I felt internally. (Of course, I knew it was actually my job to perform for thousands of people and deliver a high standard, but it was not helpful for me to think about this reality.)*

According to recent research, dancers who regularly experience flow show the following characteristics of an autotelic personality:

- They are eager for challenge.
- They have high-level concentration skills.
- They are intrinsically motivated.
- They engage in active coping strategies. (Jaque et al., 2020)

> *When encountering a challenge, I try to be radical. Often when we are challenged or try new things, we get very conservative, get cold feet and return to our default. So I constantly try to move my attention to sensation and focus, almost trying to be more primal.*

Dancers with autotelic personality types also possess meta-skills such as general curiosity, persistence and low self-centeredness (Csíkszentmihályi, 1990).

> *I was endlessly curious in myriad ways – creative, musical, literary, philosophical, psychological – constantly learning and constantly examining how they influenced (or might influence) dancing, artistry, expressivity and me as a performing artist.*

These individuals generally have personalities with lower anxiety and higher self-esteem (Asakawa, 2009). Their strong self-esteem may give them enough confidence to risk 'losing themselves' in performance.

> *When I am portraying a character, it is easy for me to get lost in who that character is, how they react to others and express themselves. This is often fun and calming because I feel as surprised or intrigued by my character's experience as I assume an audience member would be, lost in the moment.*

Similarly, lower trait anxiety may make them unafraid to explore new possibilities and enable them to simply let things unfold.

> *It's a learning experience, and it's an art form, so setting aside a space for the unexpected to happen within a performance is important. The space to let it be. To let go of expectations is a helpful approach in performance. Then the mind can relax.*

A few of the responding dancers refer to the experience of a 'blank mind' or a 'clear and conscious mind, like meditation'. Generally, the term *blank mind* has negative connotations, but these dancers refer to a situation like a meditative state, where cognition (conscious thought) disappears.

> *When I feel a sense of harmony in a performance, class or rehearsal, it is usually because there is an absence of thought and I am emotionally and physically connected to the music, my partner, the story and the movement. The feeling is euphoric, and I feel completely present in that very moment.*

With a 'blank mind', sensations, emotions and images are heightened, thereby magnifying the performance experience.

> *In the blank mind state, there's a natural integration/coherence between all these different sensations: the movements, the music, your surroundings and how you feel internally.*

Although rarely mentioned in academic discussion of 'flow', several dancers reported experiences marked by a deep sense of honesty or truth. Possibly the overwhelming focus on intrinsic motivation and reduced cognitive awareness leaves the dancer's inner self open and free to express itself.

> *It's one of those feelings that is quite hard to describe; it's a feeling of elation like you have reached the highest point of what it means to be true to yourself.*

Voluntary extra-corporeal (out of body) experiences occur when a person voluntarily produces internal somatosensory experiences as if they were occurring outside their own body. Smith and Messier say that 'the experience is accompanied by a profound feeling of being outside of the body and with feelings of meaningfulness of the experience' (Smith & Messier, 2014). They suggest that the experience may be relatively widespread but remain unreported because the subjects do not realise it is unusual. One dancer described the experience as being of benefit to their performance.

> *In performance especially, I would sometimes have this sense that I could see myself. Especially my face. It's hard to explain this one. It's almost like you are looking at your face. Aware of your facial expressions but not controlling them. (Weird.) But this was something I did as a child too. It helped me feel present and out of my head.*

In another dancer's words,

> *It feels like being someone else. Almost floating above yourself, watching yourself dance. For some reason, on the rare occasion I feel this, I see myself dancing from behind and from a slightly elevated viewpoint and have the sensation that time is slowed down and that I have total control.*

In a study of the physiological aspects of flow while playing the piano, researchers noted that increased flow correlated with conditions associated with increased attention and arousal:

- Decreased heart period (time between heart muscle relaxation and contraction);
- Increased cardiac output (quantity of blood pumped by the heart in one minute);
- Increased respiratory rate (number of breaths per minute) (de Manzano et al., 2010).

Flow can also stimulate other conditions that are not associated with cognitive or physical load:

- Increased respiratory depth (amount of air that is inhaled and exhaled);
- Increased involuntary activity of the smile muscle;
- Decreased involuntary activity of the frown muscle;
- Increased heart-rate variability (variability between the timing of successive heart beats) synchronized with respiration (de Manzano et al., 2010).

Since it was first identified by Csíkszentmihályi in the 1990s, flow has been reported in a broad range of activities. Many artists, including musicians, writers, poets and visual artists, report flow experiences.

*As a queer person I generally feel a greater sense of visibility when I perform in contemporary dance works, as they often touch on aspects of my life that classical ballet usually alienates. This really enhances my performance. I feel a greater sense of honesty.*

Nor is flow specific to the arts. Marathon competitors frequently refer to a 'runner's high', and skydivers report similar euphoric experiences. There have been a few research studies on the role of flow in surgery. For example, Dr Charles Limb, surgeon, researcher, jazz musician and amateur chef, says, 'When I'm actually operating, when I'm doing surgery, you get into this flow state where nothing else seems to matter. That flow state feels very similar to what I feel when I'm playing music. It's not the same modality, but it feels like the same brain state at times, and it's almost the same I feel when I'm cooking' (Warr et al., 2018).

Researchers investigating online gaming's overwhelming popularity cited the flow experience as part of players' attraction to the game (Nuyens et al., 2019). A year later, Khoshnoud and colleagues suggested the flow state might reduce symptoms of anxiety and depression in gamers (Khoshnoud et al., 2020). At the other end of the spectrum, in her 2006 Masters research paper, Wolfe reported anecdotal evidence of committing a crime as 'intrinsically pleasurable' for offenders, leading to a neurophysiological high resembling flow (Wolfe, 2006). Clearly, dancers can experience extraordinary joy and a sense of mastery through flow.

*It's transcendent! In a state of flow, you have power to do whatever you want – to play with technique, to express nuances in the music, to reveal a character to an audience, to make them share your character's or your own emotion.*

However, enjoyment of flow experiences is unlikely to lead to addiction in professional dancers, whose daily routine of conditioning, warm-up, class, rehearsal, preparation and performance leaves no time for the repetitive, single-focused behaviour characteristic of addiction. In fact, the contributing dancers appear to regard flow as a profound pleasure rather than a necessity. Most retiring dancers maintain a daily exercise routine, partly to maintain their physical health and partly because they enjoy it and, indeed, high-level exercise can induce flow. However, another question arises. Could the loss of relatively frequent flow experiences during performing contribute to the debilitating grief experienced by some dancers after retiring from dancing careers?

# 2 Breath, movement, emotion and music

*Emotion is obviously the reason I dance. However, it has changed roles. I have gone from entering ballet aiming to express emotion (perhaps 'dance at' an audience) to now researching emotion through allowing it to be a by-product of my action. This means allowing the movement to come first and listening to how it triggers me emotionally, so it's a curious process of research.*

Ballet is much more than skills, as this quote and many others throughout this book make abundantly clear. In general, successful dancers see dancing and performing as a fusion of movement, emotion, creativity and artistry: they want to express beauty and abstract ideas through movement; they want to share the emotion and the sensory experiences of the movement itself and of the roles they play. In pursuing their goals, they explore a process known as embodiment. Dance is sometimes held up as the ultimate expression of embodiment, which can be described as awareness of the body and mind as an integrated whole. Gomes and colleagues (2021) describe the two-way nature of embodiment research: to understand how body movements contribute to thought and emotion, and how thought and emotion influence movement. Embodiment is believed to be 'shaped by the person's attitudes, beliefs, experience and learning in a social and cultural context' (Mehling et al., 2009). For dancers, embodiment describes their experience of dance as a multi-layered process, involving not only their bodies but also their thoughts, emotions and intentions.

*It feels like I can rely on my instincts to make artistic and physical choices and my body knows exactly what it needs to do to make it work, without hesitating.*

For most dancers, emotion and movement are tightly bound with music, and the symbiotic relationship between them has been researched extensively. Each of the three is linked directly with the other two, with respiration strengthening each link. The following diagram illustrates this concept, with dance as the outcome.

We feel emotion throughout the day, be it pleasure on seeing a friend, annoyance at a dirty mark on a clean jacket or anxiety at being late for a meeting. However, emotion plays a much more important role in our lives. Early in human evolution, our brains evolved to 'optimise our survival, and to allow us to flourish' (Immordino-Yang & Damasio, 2011), and emotions emerged at a later stage to 'motivate action to benefit the organism' (Damasio, 2019). For example, fear motivates a creature to move away from danger, while the possibility of pleasure entices it to move closer. Emotion influences almost every action we make – whether, when and how we perform it. Williams and colleagues expanded on this by saying, 'All actions have a motivation or an emotional value, which results in the action

12  *Unveiling dancers' artistry*

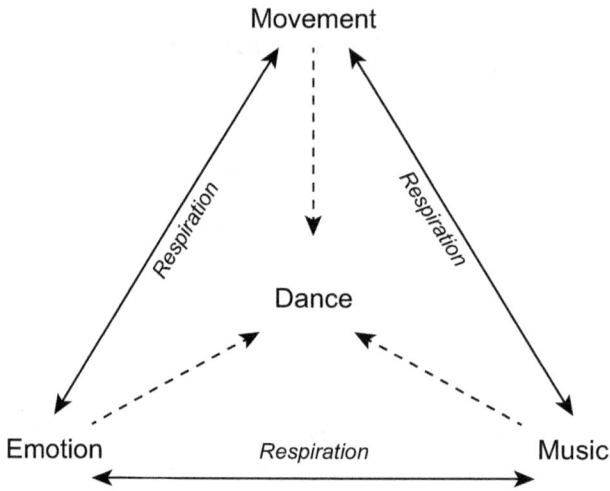

*Figure 2.1* Components of dance.
Source: diagram after Bernardi et al., 2017.

being planned to achieve a desirable goal' (Williams et al., 2020). When emotion motivates an action, sensory feedback informs the motor system whether the action is achieving its goal. Dancing and all other voluntary movements are regulated by the sensorimotor system, which integrates cognitive intention with movement, emotion and the senses. Ramachandran and Altschuler describe a network of connections 'from sensory input to both the cognitive regions of the brain and the emotional processing regions of the brain' (Ramachandran & Altschuler, 2009).

Fascinatingly, this neuroscientific perspective is reflected in the quote at the top of this chapter. The dancer describes their own creative journey, from 'dancing at' the audience to 'allowing the movement to come first and listening to how it triggers me emotionally'. Moors and Fischer say that the complexity of human actions is due to the existence of subjective awareness – conscious awareness of our own emotional experiences. In their words, 'Subjective awareness allows humans to consciously control how emotions are expressed through action, resulting in greater variability of emotional expressions, as well as variability in how emotions influence actions and decision making' (Moors & Fischer, 2018). Subjective awareness allows dancers to finetune and vary the emotional impact of their performances.

> Although performing may appear to be unrelated to scientific research, dancers can devote their whole career to exploring, or researching, the expressive potential of the human body.

While emotion helps regulate an animal's or a person's own behaviour, their emotion also assists survival by influencing the behaviour of others (Williams et al., 2020). According to

Moors and Fischer, 'We manifest our inner intentions, dispositions and thoughts by means of overt behaviour. Similarly, we try to figure out the intentions, dispositions and thoughts of others, when witnessing their behaviour' (Moors & Fischer, 2018) Understanding another person's inner state allows us to predict their actions and to respond appropriately. Dogs, like other higher animals, have elaborate approach rituals designed to assess the emotion and intention of other dogs – they may approach sideways, dip their heads and drop their ears to establish a friendly, nonconfrontational relationship. Humans also convey their emotion and their intention through their faces and bodies, from the pantomime aggression of professional wrestlers to the delicate, silent interaction between two shy but mutually attracted people. Professor Peggy Mason of the University of Chicago reported a revealing instance of the power of emotion over voluntary control. A patient suffered a stroke that prevented voluntary movement of one side of her face, regardless of whether she tried to move it herself or her physician asked her to do so. However, the physician told a funny joke and the patient smiled naturally, activating both sides of her face equally. Professor Mason concluded, 'We embody our emotion, and we embody it both in our facial expressions and in our postures' (Mason, 2022).

While our brains originally evolved 'to manage our physiology, to optimize our survival, and to allow us to flourish', Williams and his colleagues remarked that 'emotions, which play out in the body and mind, are profoundly intertwined with thought' (Williams et al., 2020). This interplay between emotions, body and the mind lies at the heart of elite dancers' performance.

> *When I acknowledge that my emotions – and all parts of me – can have a helpful place in my dancing, it helps me feel more myself, and makes the movement feel more natural.*

The word *motion* developed from the old French word *mouvoir* ('to move' in a physical sense), while the word *emotion* emerged later to mean a disturbance within the body, possibly tears or laughter. The link between physical motion and emotions is evident in several languages. In English, we may be 'moved' physically or emotionally; we feel 'pushed' to meet a deadline; friends 'stick together'; we can feel 'bogged down' with work; a phone call may give us a 'lift' or make us feel 'down'. The movement aspect of these metaphors is a perfect representation of our emotions. The question of whether emotion emanates from the physical body or the mind has been debated for centuries. These days, technological advances in measuring blood flow through the brain and body show close associations between body sensations and emotions (Nummenmaa et al., 2013). This association is captured in a dancer's perceptive comment:

> *Emotion can actually be produced through movement for me. Movement, and what I create with my movement, can 'become' an emotion. Through tapping into the senses.*

Dancers may benefit by exploring the connection between a particular movement and the emotion it evokes, or the way an emotion affects a certain movement. One of the contributing dancers reported dancing better in class when feeling sad, possibly because sadness dampened their frequently heightened anxiety. The ongoing conversation between our own imagery, sensations, actions and emotions reveals our capacity to communicate more richly than through words, and possibly with a greater insight than through our conscious mind.

> Young dancers are often told to 'leave their emotions at the door', presumably so they will be compliant in the studio. How can a habit of repressing emotions on a regular basis help a young dancer become an emotionally expressive artist?

Although humans are natural experts in expressing their emotions through their bodies, it is difficult to fake emotions convincingly. In 1862, the French anatomist GB Duchenne first defined the differences between fake smiles and smiles resulting from true enjoyment or pleasure. In his honour, genuine smiles have been identified as Duchenne smiles ever since. Bogodistov and Dost showed that both Duchenne and non-Duchenne (fake) smiles engage the zygomatic major muscles to lift the corners of the mouth (Bogodistov & Dost, 2017). However, only Duchenne smiles activate the orbicularis oculi muscles, which pull up the cheeks and create or deepen wrinkles around the outside of the eyes (crow's feet). Only Duchenne smiles are accompanied by activity in the brain region involved in experiencing enjoyment. Well-practised fake smiles can mimic some of the more obvious characteristics of a Duchenne smile, but not the additional Duchenne markers of a very slight lowering of the eyebrows, with the skin above the eyes being pulled slightly downward. Evolution has ensured we sense discrepancies in fake smiles and usually react with a sense of unease or distrust. Our ability to recognise any mismatch between smiles, words and actions makes us less likely to be convinced by non-Duchenne smiles.

Over the past decades, researchers have examined whether fake smiles can, in turn, influence the smiler's emotional state – whether fake smiles can make people happier. Strack and his colleagues showed that subjects found cartoons slightly funnier when they activated their zygomatic major (smile) muscles by holding a pen sideways between their teeth (Strack et al., 1988). Larsen and his colleagues asked subjects to hold a pen at right angles to their teeth (pointing forward) and 'attempt to manipulate golf tees attached to their foreheads in such a way as to mimic a sad emotional face pattern' (Larsen et al., 1992). Unsurprisingly, these poor subjects produced unconvincing results. Matsumoto argued against the findings of similar research papers, saying that 'the effect of facial feedback on emotional experience is less than convincing' (Matsumoto, 1987). However, media promotion of the benefit of fake smiles to the fake smiler led to social acceptance of this flawed concept, and it became rampant in the ballet world.

> Many ballet students are encouraged to smile in class, possibly to indicate enjoyment or to please the teacher or a potential examiner. In fact, each student will experience a range of emotions during class, at times being inspired by the music or the exercise itself, concerned about technical issues or distracted by the teacher, other students and personal issues. Since the likelihood of a genuine smile lasting throughout class is minimal, these students are forced to adopt non-Duchenne smiles. An entrenched link between dancing and a fake smile can be hard to break, especially if it persists into the profession. Unfortunately, fake smiling can interrupt the natural connection between movement and true emotion, making the dancer less expressive.

Fake smiling can have a negative impact on emotional wellbeing. Grandey and Sayre showed a correlation between employees who are required to smile at work and a high degree of heavy drinking. They concluded that 'effortfully amplifying, faking, and suppressing emotional expressions' is harmful for employees' emotional health. (Grandey & Sayre, 2019) Another study explored the experiences of female nurses of colour who work in predominantly white hospitals in the United States (Cottingham et al., 2017). The study showed these nurses experience an emotional 'double shift', due to the pressures of continually smiling to avoid daily microaggressions from white patients, combined with the need to smile in the nurses' rest areas to avoid similar microaggressions from white members of staff. Again, the nurses' continual fake smiling was shown to be damaging to their mental and emotional health.

Music and movement are the other two elements in the 'Components of Dance' diagram. For many dancers, music and dance are inseparable, and research reveals a close relationship between the two. Levitin and Tirovolas remarked that music cannot exist without movement, because physical motion is required to set sound-producing molecules in motion (Levitin & Tirovolas, 2009). They used fMRI to study activation in the brain's motor (movement) areas when participants lay completely still while listening to music. They found that the brain's motor areas were activated regardless of the participants' lack of visible movement. Levitin commented, 'It's as if movement is impossible to suppress'. Levitin's remark will not surprise women who have felt their unborn babies kick, squirm or quieten in response to certain music. Nor will parents be surprised by research showing that very young babies can detect a regular beat and enjoy being bounced to rhythmic music (Phillips-Silver & Trainor, 2005). Perhaps more surprising, regular rhythm appears to be related to social behaviour.

Cirelli and colleagues showed that 14-month-old toddlers were helpful and cooperative with researchers who had previously bounced in rhythm with them and the accompanying music. Conversely, the toddlers showed no interest in cooperating with researchers who had intentionally bounced out of time with them and the music (Cirelli et al., 2014). Other researchers showed that 'children who participated in a musical game later played together in a more helpful and cooperative manner than children who participated in a non-musical game.' (Kirschner & Tomasello, 2010). Movement synchrony may possibly help identify others 'like me' and so promote social bonding. This instinct, which appears to be innate, may support the popularity of group activities such as communal singing, social dancing and crowds swaying in unison at concerts and sports. Marching, commonly regarded as a means of forming and displaying group cohesion, may demand regimented bearing, lines and spacing. When this is accompanied by synchronised head and eye movement, the resulting impression of almost robotic control may be used to depict unanimity of purpose, possibly of protection or of threat. Movement synchrony could also underlie 'the camaraderie of the corps de ballet', where the pleasure of moving as one in response to music can foster a sense of cohesion among the dancers – at least in the short term.

While music's pulse urges us to move physically, music also contains movement within itself – 'patterns of tension and relaxation, impressions of rushing forwards and pulling back, of advancing inch by inch or vaulting great distances, of expanding outwards and contracting' as well as other patterns of movement (Carroll & Moore, 2008). These researchers claim that 'some dance is best understood as the clarification or deepening of the feelings of movement inspired by the music, and that this clarification or deepening is secured, in part, by the activation of the motor reflexes in the body of the spectator'. Carroll and Moore's statement is supported by many dancers' experiences, as they search to coordinate the dynamic within the music with the dynamic in their own body, the choreography and other dancers.

> *Musicality was always the driver of movement for me. If you take notice of the accents, rhythm, tone and style of the music, it tells you what to do and when to do it. Technique and musicality are really intertwined for me. The music can determine how you are going to express a movement and what dynamics you use.*

Since many studies show that moving 'on the beat' is present from early babyhood, it is generally considered to be innate and universal, but this does not take away from the fact that moving in time with a musical rhythm is a complicated process. The brain must first recognise the regularity of the beats in a sequence and must then predict when the next beat will occur (Merchant et al., 2015). This prediction is generally believed to involve both sensory and motor systems.

> *The music could initiate a physical response in me and drive my movement. I would react to the music. I actually felt as if I would almost chase the music. As if my bones were pulled by the music, and then the movement happened.*

Bernardi and colleagues observed, 'Listening to music is a complex phenomenon, involving psychological, emotional, neurological, and cardiovascular changes, with behavioural modifications of breathing' (Bernardi et al., 2005). Soon after, Zatorre and colleagues reported that areas of the motor system are involved in musical timing, sequencing, pitch and rhythm (Zatorre et al., 2007). While examining whether a specific respiration state could be indicator of a specific emotion, Noguchi and colleagues measured respiratory and cardiovascular (heart and blood flow) patterns while participants were listening to music by Stockhausen and music by Chopin (Noguchi et al., 2012). When listening to Stockhausen's composition, participants reported negative emotions like anger and fear, and these were accompanied by a rapid, shallow respiratory rate, alertness and arousal – all signs the body was preparing to defend itself. Chopin's music, on the other hand, induced a positive emotional state and a sense of comfort, with a decrease in respiratory rate. Later, Sakaguchi and Aiba noted that breathing, which depends on the contraction and relaxation of the diaphragm, cannot be independent from motor control and body movement (Sakaguchi & Aiba, 2016). The strong links between music, respiration, movement and emotion form a perfect crucible for dance.

> Music is the shorthand of emotion. Emotions, which let themselves be described in words with such difficulty, are directly conveyed to man in music, and in that is its power and significance.
>
> Leo Tolstoy, in *The Kreutzer Sonata*

Music may convey emotion in two ways (Juslin & Laukka, 2010). We may 'perceive' (recognize) emotion in the music, or the music may 'induce' (create) emotion in us. Perceiving or recognising emotion is a cognitive (thinking) process that may not necessarily cause an emotional experience, whereas inducing an emotion means we experience or 'feel' it. Although music frequently induces simple emotions such as happiness and sadness, it seems to be less effective at inducing more complex emotions like jealousy and dishonesty. Dancers need to express a diverse and nuanced range of emotions in performance, but, in their case, emotions expressed through the music are enhanced by the expressive power of their bodies, their faces and the choreographed gestures and movements.

*I feel the way my whole body bends, stretches and coordinates like a whole instrument, reaching out into the space around me.*

Music influences dancers in a multitude of ways. Some dancers seem to rely on the music to sustain and excite them, raising the question of whether they would have pursued a ballet career for dance alone.

*I have always thought of dance as music made visible. I believe that dance is an extension of music, music is almost an imitation of what's inside making itself manifest on the outside.*

George Balanchine, a Russian-American choreographer who trained as a concert pianist and later co-founded New York City Ballet, was known for perfectly aligning the steps and choreographic design with the musical score. His approach to musicality in dance places the dancer as a servant of the music.

*Music is essential to me. It makes the movement. Balanchine used to say he should see the music and hear the dance.*

One dancer could find the beauty of the music almost overwhelming.

*Sometimes, I loved the music so much – it was so exquisite – that I just didn't feel worthy of it. This put me in a terrible space psychologically. I just didn't measure up.*

For another, music and dance are almost playmates in creating each class and performance.

*I love playing with the music and with phrasing the movements, exploring different possibilities each night. At best, I feel a symbiotic relationship between the music and my movement, and I love merging with the tiny differences in the conductor's or pianist's approach each day.*

Many dancers rely on the music to guide and inspire their technical skills.

*Using the rhythm, the emotion of the music greatly improves your movement quality and technique as you use the impulses at the right times.*

But, for most dancers, music, emotion and movement are one.

*When my mind, my emotions, the music and my body are in harmony, it feels like freedom – I can dance with real abandon.*

Respiration, or breathing, can be seen in the 'Components of Dance' diagram as strengthening the links between emotion, movement and music. Breathing is normally automatic, varying in response to feedback from a complex network of nerves monitoring the state of the body. It is regulated primarily to support the chemical processes producing the energy required to support the body's functions, and to maintain the body in optimal conditions for survival. However, breathing is also fundamental to expressive actions such as speaking, singing and playing musical instruments, and its role in dance is to act as the coordinating factor between movement, emotion and music. De Melo and colleagues examined the influence of emotions on people's breathing (de Melo et al., 2010). They programmed virtual humans with a range of different breathing patterns, each related to a different emotion. Participants were able to identify those related to excitement, pain, relief, anger, fear, panic, boredom and startle, purely by observing the virtual humans' respiration patterns. Surprisingly, relaxation, disgust, surprise, sadness and joy were more difficult to identify from programmed breathing patterns in this research. While breathing is influenced by emotion, it also influences emotion in 'a bi-directional relationship between the body and the mind' (Jerath & Beveridge, 2020). Damasio and Carvalho describe emotions as innate action programs, aimed at changing the way the body interacts with the environment in order to maintain or restore the body's optimal state (Damasio & Carvalho, 2013). The relationship between body sensations and emotions draws the brain's attention to any threat to the body's survival, such as hunger, cold or pain.

> Dancers facing the difficulties of technical training frequently hold their breath, then take a quick inhalation to help them manage the next challenge. Strategies like these interfere with the body's automatic control of such vital factors as oxygen levels, lung pressure, heart rate and respiratory muscle contractions. They also interfere with emotions and movement control.

It is essential for dancers' physical wellbeing and for their dancing that they develop healthy breathing patterns. These patterns form a stable background for any short-term breathing changes needed to support exceptional exertion. Coordination of breath with movement is key to advancing dancers' technical development and emotional expressivity.

*Before entering the stage, I would breathe very slowly and concentrate on relaxing as much as I could. This would bring me into the zone where I needed to be. To not think but simply let my body carry me through each movement as if it was completely new.*

# 3 Expressivity, harmony, creativity and artistry

Expressivity, or the capacity to express emotions, music, characters and ideas through movement, is an essential quality in a successful dancer. The specific choreography, the music, the theme or story, the costume and the stage design provide stimuli for a dancer's artistry, but the ability to express artistry naturally and convincingly through the dancing body's movement and technique is learned. The concept of body expressivity is not new. In 1872, Charles Darwin wrote *The Expression of the Emotions in Man and Animals*, his third book on evolutionary theory (Darwin, 2018). In 1890, the philosopher William James explored the recognition of emotion in whole-body posture in *The Principles of Psychology*, an equally influential work (James, 1890). However, most early investigations focused on subjects' facial reactions to stereotypical depictions of fear, anger, sadness and joy. Possibly the focus on facial expressions evolved because the body was often obscured by 19th-century clothing, possibly because facial emotion is an important feature in literature and in visual art of the period and possibly because faces are more frequently seen and so might be easier to study. Nevertheless, Aviezer and colleagues compared the relative expressivity of faces and bodies. Their research involved photographs of the faces and bodies of people undergoing intensely positive emotions (e.g., winning an international tennis match) and intensely negative emotions (e.g., during nipple-piercing) (Aviezer et al., 2012). The accuracy of participants' evaluation of facial emotions was poor, but their accuracy increased when they saw the body and face together, or even the body alone. Next, the researchers created a completely new set of photographs by pasting negative faces onto photos of positive bodies, and vice versa. The participants, who were unaware of the photo manipulation, unconsciously based their evaluations on the bodies rather than the faces. Studies by other researchers have found similar results – viewers are more inclined to believe emotions expressed by the body, trusting them more than facial expressions. As a primitive survival mechanism, this would make sense. A stranger might hide his hunting knife from view while approaching another group. With luck, an astute potential victim might see beyond the stranger's friendly smile to recognise treachery in his unconscious 'body language'.

There appear to be differences in brain activity when expressing emotion through the face or through the body. Enea and Iancu showed that emotion expressed through the body activates a range of motor areas that are not active during facial expression of emotion (Enea & Iancu, 2015). Aviezer and colleagues reported that although faces and bodies 'often convey some of the same information; when they do not, it is oftentimes the body that reveals the expressers' genuine feelings' (Aviezer et al., 2012). As observers, we are usually able to spot a lie.

DOI: 10.4324/9781003395188-5

> This information can be invaluable for dancers, who may underestimate the expressive power of their own bodies and the need for emotional honesty. Young dancers who have been encouraged to 'act with their faces' may benefit from knowing that audiences will be more convinced by the emotion expressed through their bodies.

Taking a different approach, Nummenmaa and colleagues asked participants from a range of cultures to record where they 'felt' a physical response when they experienced each of thirteen different emotions (Nummenmaa et al., 2013). The resulting body maps were consistent between individuals and across cultural backgrounds, indicating that physical responses to emotion are universal. Happiness was accompanied by strong activation in the head and heart area, followed by lesser but still noticeable activation throughout the body. Anger focused activation in the lower arms and fists, while sadness evoked weak activation in the eyes, throat and heart and very little or no activation elsewhere in the body. It is hypothesised that these emotion-triggered activations prepare the body to respond appropriately – happiness fills the body with positive energy, anger prepares the body to fight and sadness leaves energy at a low ebb. The strong relationship between emotion and physical response is reflected in colloquial expressions across language groups. In English, we feel 'sick to the stomach' with disgust, we 'tremble with delight' and we 'glow with pride'. In other words, the two-way relationship between emotion and the body was recognised in language long before science proved it to be so.

Neither students nor professional dancers come to class as emotional 'blank slates'. Circumstances, events, conversations, personal health and the weather can colour the way they feel as they enter the studio, and their mood may influence their personal and technical responses in class. To avoid disruption, teachers often tell students to 'leave your emotions at the door'. This approach may help maintain a calm class atmosphere, but long-term damage may be done. The network of neural connections linking imagery, sensations, emotions and movement can become fragmented if emotion is disconnected from movement on a regular basis. Even so-called negative emotions can play a role in class – the sensorimotor aspects of spite and anger can give new dimensions to *battements frappés*!

> Young dancers spend countless hours working on their technique, hoping to make their movements both precise and beautiful. However, technique must be more than that. A dancer's technique must be as expressive as every other movement they make.

Healthy young children express every emotion and thought throughout their bodies. Joy, hope and disappointment can be seen in their energy flow, the way their limbs move, the way they breathe, their dynamics and their coordination. We feel their emotions deep within ourselves as we share the sensations of their movement. Ideally, this precious synthesis of body, movement and emotion is at the core of ballet and is the goal of successful dancers in any field.

*Expressivity, harmony, creativity and artistry* 21

> *Emotion permeating the movement, rather than being on top of it, is my own process of artistic development. It was usually my body and soul that led me in my dancing. Emotion was not there at the beginning usually. It was sensing my bones, my skin, my centre of being that led me creatively.*

Unfortunately, social pressure and media influence can replace the beauty of children's naïve movement with something more socially acceptable. Children who learn ballet can rein in their innate movement as they try to make their bodies conform to a highly specialized technique and an adult aesthetic. They can become pre-occupied with thinking, remembering and achieving exercises and steps and, in the process, they can lose the fundamental ingredients of expressive technique.

> *When I was younger, I saw my body more as a piece of machinery that I was trying to adjust and shape in a particular way. Recently I've found that the more I acknowledge what I'm feeling and notice how these feelings present in my body throughout each day, the more I am in touch with the true nature of my body: an expressive instrument.*

The dancer's observation at the beginning of this chapter is evidence of the fact that, for many dancers, emotion emanates from within movement. The profound connection

*Figure 3.1* La Bayadère.
*Source*: https://commons.wikimedia.org/wiki/File:Labayaderewhiteact.jpg.

between movement and emotion is second nature to children who want to dance, but it should be conserved as a precious resource throughout the introduction of technical concepts and, indeed, throughout training in every form of dance. By awakening and developing somatic awareness, the young dancer learns to express emotion and creativity through all movement, including technical exercises and dance in general.

The sense of harmony is not widely discussed in dance, even though it is clearly important to the dancers who contributed to this book. In non-musical terms, *harmony* refers to a sense of balance, unity and beauty created by a particular arrangement of two or more elements. In dance, harmony may lie in the coordination of the body's movements, breathing and energy with their intention and meaning, or in the coordination between dancers. As an example, the entrance of the 'Shades' in *La Bayadère*, with its mesmerising repetition of dream-like arabesques, produces a prolonged state of harmony. Although dance can be deeply harmonious in itself, music, lighting and staging can blend with movement to create harmony between all elements. As can be seen in the quote that follows, harmony is deeply satisfying for dancers. It may also be the most satisfying gift that audiences receive from dancers.

> *Harmony between your body, the movement and the music can bring a real sense of joy: an implicit sense of surrender and ecstasy. In these moments, there's also an awareness which is actually hard to describe, that 'you' – an essence of you – is alive, felt, and present in the movement.*

While some degree of harmony between brain and body is a natural product of evolution, dancers need to expand and fine-tune the network of links between the sensorimotor system, thinking, imagery, movement, music and emotion to achieve harmony in performance. In general, dancers acknowledge that their own thought processes can contribute to or stand in the way of a harmonious performance.

> *When I feel a sense of harmony in a performance, class or rehearsal, it is usually because there is an absence of thought and I am emotionally and physically connected to the music, my partner, the story and the movement. The feeling is euphoric, and I feel completely present in that very moment.*

Achieving harmony can be an absorbing lifelong pursuit for dancers in any genre, while creating and disrupting harmony can add light and shade to any performance. The ability of choreographers like Wayne MacGregor to manipulate and challenge our expectations of harmony has stretched audiences' concept of ballet as an expressive art form.

Given its worldwide importance in the arts, technology, the sciences and business, it may be surprising that the concept of creativity was not defined until Morris Stein wrote a journal article about inventive ideas (Stein, 1953). Before then, achievements we now might attribute to creativity were assigned to genius or divine inspiration, but Stein's wish to avoid these attributions led him to devise the new term. The concept of creativity quickly gained acceptance and, decades later, Runco and Jaeger established a definitive statement, namely 'Creativity requires both originality and effectiveness' (Runco & Jaeger, 2012). Since the nature of creativity adapts to the requirements of each discipline, various researchers have described how these priorities operate in the arts. The most succinct are:

- Originality: 'expressing the personally and culturally idiosyncratic self' (Margolis, 1981);
- Effectiveness: 'insight' (Sawyer, 2011).

*Expressivity, harmony, creativity and artistry* 23

*Figure 3.2* Dyad (1929). Choreography: Wayne McGregor in (2009). Dancers: Robyn Hendricks and Daniel Gaudiello. Lighting and co-set design: Lucy Carter.
*Source*: Photograph by Jim McFarlane, courtesy of The Australian Ballet.

Margolis' reference to the personal, cultural and idiosyncratic nature of creativity reveals the depth of the term *originality*, while Sawyer's 'insight' takes creativity far beyond simple novelty. Other researchers have redefined creativity but, regardless of the specific words chosen, there is a consensus that originality and effectiveness lie at its core. Free and improvised dance styles such as contact improvisation, interpretive dance and street dance are based on natural movement skills and expression rather than formal techniques, so one might expect these dancers to be more creative than dancers in formalised techniques like ballet or Bharatanatyam. Overall, free dancers devote their creativity to developing the movement itself as well as its musical or rhythmic and expressive qualities. For those working in styles with techniques such as classical ballet, where the basic movement vocabulary is already defined, each dancer's creativity lies in their ability to express emotion, ideas and the music through their idiosyncratic movement quality. Each dancer's body is unique, so each dancer's movement must be unique. Each person's unique combination of skeletal structure, soft tissue structure and strength, together with their individual sensory and motor control mechanisms, ensures that any given movement will differ from person to person. Add to this the fact that our motor systems can never repeat our own movements accurately, and we can see that technical rules can never produce absolute conformity between repetitions or between dancers. This inevitable variability gives the dancer endless opportunities to explore the new sensory, musical and emotional potential of a movement each time they perform it. Exploration facilitates creativity. By identifying, even subconsciously, a range of movement approaches that might meet personal and expressive criteria in various circumstances, dancers expand their creative range. Contrary to the idea that creative mental ideas lead to actions that appear to be creative, Orth and colleagues (2017) propose that 'creative solutions emerge in the act rather than before'. This argument aligns perfectly with the experiences of many dancers.

> *Other than the 'steps' being choreographed already, everything else was up to me to play with.*

Creativity in classwork may be seen in the way a dancer coordinates their body parts, or phrases the various elements of the movement, such as respiration, coordination, dynamics and punctuation. A slight anticipation with the eyes, a languorous delay in the head movement, a light breath to accentuate a movement's dynamics – such small changes can bring creativity to any movement, from *battements frappés* to *petit allegro* to a *grand pas de deux*. Even exercises in class can inspire a range of emotions. An *adage* might be dreamy or passionate, while it's impossible to be miserable during any *allegro* – upset or angry, possibly, but not miserable. This is even more the case in rehearsals and performances, when the choreography and the music together create the emotion the choreographer wants to express. Creativity is triggered by imagination. Imagining the ebbing and flowing of waves on the shore can make a series of *ronds de jambe* a creative sensory experience for the dancer and for the viewer. Imagery can facilitate creativity in class, rehearsal and performance, while both creativity and imagery are core ingredients in the development of artistry.

Artistry is recognised as a core aspect of the arts in general, with minor variations in the defining criteria within each art form. The criteria for artistry in dance as a performing art have broadened over the past two centuries, firstly in response to the growing diversity of ballet in the western world and then to encompass the broad range of more recent developments in dance. Ballet is a specific genre within dance, ranging from classical ballet's identifiable technique and style, which were consolidated in the 19th century, to new exploitation of the technique's physical and aesthetic potential.

In the 17th century, King Louis XIV of France chose ballet as the ideal vehicle to demonstrate his complete mastery of the known world. His role as monarch was already embodied in his magnificent Palace of Versailles, which is surrounded by chateaux, formal gardens, sculptures, fountains and ornamental lakes stretching beyond the horizon in every direction, and he complemented this magnificence with grand spectacles of ballet, music, acting and poetry.

Louis followed the classical aesthetic ideals of ancient Greece and Rome, namely simplicity, harmony, balance, clarity, restraint, unity and proportion, with *proportion* referring to an ideal balance between design elements or, in human terms, between parts of the body and symmetry of the body as a whole. These ideals were believed to lead to beauty, which was placed alongside truth and goodness as one of the three highest goals a cultivated person could pursue. Johan Winckelmann, an 18th-century German art historian, said that beauty relies on beauty of form, beauty of an idea and beauty of expression, stressing that beauty is felt by the senses but understood and created by the intellect (Winckelmann, 1972). For thousands of years, classical ideals have inspired artists to produce works of extraordinary beauty, such as the Colosseum (80AD) and the second act of *Swan Lake* by Lev Ivanov (1895).

*Expressivity, harmony, creativity and artistry* 25

*Figure 3.3* The Palace at Versailles with elaborate ornamental gardens ranging beyond the horizon.
*Source*: Paolo Costa Baldi, CC BY-SA 3.0, via Wikimedia Commons.

In classical ballet technique, unfortunately, some misinterpret the overarching goal of 'mastery' as 'perfection'. As a result, the search for geometric perfection has often been placed ahead of the reality of human bodies, quite frequently resulting in physical as well as psychological harm. In fact, classical ideals aim for beauty of the mind as well as the body, with the intention of bringing the viewer intense aesthetic pleasure and intellectual satisfaction.

Definitions within the arts are necessarily subjective, coloured by the artist's or observer's professional experiences and personal approach. In general, the goal of artistry is to share, to reveal or to inspire unique insights emerging from the juxtaposition of the individual dancer's personality and life experience with that of fellow artists, the choreography, music, design. Within this framework, the dancer aims to create a fluid and harmonious balance between creativity, meaning and emotional honesty. By fine-tuning these elements in different ways, each performance acquires a unique expressive identity, revealing the potential hidden within the choreography and within the role itself. Although an audience member may see numerous performances of a particular ballet, each performance should be a new journey of discovery for dancer and audience alike.

> *Artistry is a constant process of creation and intellect of, not only the brain, but intellect of the body. My body is my brain.*

26  *Unveiling dancers' artistry*

*Figure 3.4* The Colosseum in Rome, built in 80AD, with the repetitious curving arches of Roman architecture.

*Source*: Creative Commons. "Colosseum" by Javier Vieras is licensed under CC BY 2.0.

*Figure 3.5* Swan Lake. Choreography: Stephen Baynes (2012). Design: Hugh Colman. Lighting design: Rachel Burke. Artists of The Australian Ballet.

*Source*: Photographer: Daniel Boud. Courtesy of The Australian Ballet.

In contrast to this dancer's perceptive words, most dictionaries confine their definitions of artistry to skill and virtuosity. A welcome exception is Charles Annandale's *The Large Type Concise English Dictionary* (1843–1915), which describes art as 'an expression of the emotions and creative imagination in terms of line, form and colour; or in sound, gesture and rhythmic movement'. It is interesting and disappointing that this dictionary, published in the first decade of the 20th century, presents a more detailed and nuanced description than later references. According to Webster's Dictionary, artistry is 'the artistic quality of effect or workmanship' – a surprisingly circular definition that underlines the difficulty in pinpointing its exact nature. The dearth of appropriate definitions for artistry impoverishes the understanding of critics, reviewers and journalists, and so it is detrimental to the development of dance in general. Fortunately, amid the inadequate definitions of artistry, dancer/anthropologist Anya Peterson Royce said, 'Virtuosity in and of itself does not produce artistry, even though it is a necessary feature of artistic skill. Artistry, rather, is the ability to produce an interpretation that appears inevitable' (Royce, 2002) An apparently inevitable interpretation is highly valued because it arises from a cohesive, logical development of all the components of the dance or the performance. At best, a seemingly inevitable interpretation can surprise both dancer and viewer by evoking new insight and a new sense of harmony. Despite the difficulty of defining artistry, many dancers have no doubt what it is.

> *Exploring how to get the most out of the role, how the music, the meaning, breathing, phrasing and modulation of energy, all change my performance and, I believe, what the audience receives.*

Other descriptions seem to refer to inspiration, where the mind spontaneously integrates information and experiences to produce a new idea or action.

> *Sometimes artistry was what felt right in that moment, so not a choice at all, quite spontaneous, as if my movements and expression came from somewhere mysterious. As if I was just the messenger, and the story came from someone else.*

On the other hand, some dancers feel artistry comes from deep within the body.

> *Sensing the body and moving from the core is a huge aspect of artistry, because the core is your unique centre where, if you can sense and move from here, the steps will not look the same as someone else's, because they have an expression now that is from you. This is artistry to me. It's truly knowing your body and having the confidence to explore it from the inside out.*

While artistry can be felt deeply within the body, it sometimes requires a conscious intention.

> *For me, artistry is both visceral, and thought out . . . created.*

Artistry is also found in small details such as directing the audience's focus.

> *It could be where the eyes look in a moment, where you put your focus. Where you put your energy – is it in your foot, hand, shoulder blade, abdomen?*

Interestingly, some dancers do not regard emotion as part of artistry.

> *Artistry is physical for me. I have never thought of it being an emotional thing, even though for a lot of people it is. I'm not saying it can't be drawn from emotion, as I do feel emotions are there at times, and can enhance the expression of a movement.*

One dancer remarked on the importance of their relationship with their partners.

> *I would say I dance at my best when I am partnering, particularly when it's a two-way street (balanced amount of lifting or weight bearing between partners). There's something so grounding about feeling another heartbeat, and it brings me right back to the present moment. Besides, focusing on someone else feels caring, and helps me get out of my own head in a warm way.*

Another dancer summarises the balance between instinct and effort lying at the heart of artistry.

> *To sum it all up, I'd have to say that my artistry was a balance of a natural instinct and work. I definitely put thought into it. A lot of thought actually, but more reflective thought. Sometimes what I felt was right was not always right, so I'd have to 'create' a little. A balance of trusting what I have and seeking out more.*

The work of finding and constantly refreshing artistry is ongoing, even in a minor variation. The dancer first explores how the variation might contribute something special to the whole performance. Should it convey a certain meaning or emotion? Should it contrast with or balance the preceding and following choreography? The dancer looks for the potential hidden within the music and the steps, especially in the connections between steps – how one might slide or explode from one movement to another.

> *I look for the qualities in the music and aim to reflect them. Fluid, light, heavy, dense, sharp, breath-like, floaty, resistant, full, subtle.*

There is often unexpected potential within a step, a way of accenting the shape or the dynamics to make the step yours, regardless of how someone else dances the variation. The dynamic possibilities of an apparently simple movement such as extending your arm are endless – a rolling wave from the armpit through the fingertips; a reaction to an unseen force pulling your wrist; a subtle, almost sneaky slither; a silent shout of success; a cry of despair.

> *to feel the dynamics, or different parts of my body, e.g., the flick of the head, swing of the arms, softness.*

While looking for the secrets hidden within the choreography, the dancer also considers the shape of the variation as a whole. Would it be better to start with a bang, skip lightly through the steps in the middle, then finish with fireworks? Would a sense of weightiness and languor add a ballerina quality, as in Raymonda's Act 3 variation? Are you keen for people to see the subtle humour in a quirky solo? Which movement intrigues you? What does the music tell you to do? Dancers perform hundreds of *glissades* every day throughout their careers, but what might be special about this particular *glissade* within the context of this variation and this music? Possibilities within the choreography are endless, but artistry also requires a sense of balance, of proportion. With all the potential a variation might offer, the dancer must select those elements that will work together to form a cohesive whole. Despite the exploration suggested here, simplicity, or apparent simplicity, is beautiful in itself. Audience members do not want to be confronted with a cryptic crossword – they want to be led, to be surprised and to feel that the final moment could not be better, that it is 'inevitable', as Anya Peterson Royce describes. Although each performance is a new creation, the thought that led to today's performance is never wasted. It will add to the rich resources that dancers use throughout their dancing lives. Dance is ephemeral, but a small detail of a specific performance may be engraved on an audience member's memory forever. At the same time, the impermanence of any one dance performance requires dancers to maintain a curious and creative mind:

*To create, but then to let it go, and then to create again.*

# 4 Technique, training and changes in dancers' brains

This chapter discusses factors specific to ballet technique, its development, the challenges it presents and the potential effects of training on dancers' brains and minds. While many of these factors also apply to contemporary dance and other dance forms, the chapter investigates some areas that are specific to ballet and its technical training. For some of the non-dance public, the words *ballet* and *technique* are almost synonymous, with both words conjuring images of unnatural body distortions, injuries and pain as much as of visions of beauty. No doubt, the fact that non-dancers would suffer injury and pain if they forced their bodies into advanced technical positions leads them to believe trained dancers suffer similarly. Some people, influenced by sensationalist films and books, picture dancers as psychologically damaged victims manipulated within a cruel system. As with all myths, there are a few historical facts in the background. This chapter discusses these facts, together with the concept of perfection and the transition from student to professional. Given the intense training and performance schedules most students and dancers undertake to achieve their technical goals, it is not surprising that positive and negative changes have also been identified in dancers' brains and minds.

France's King Louis XIV was fascinated with ballet from a young age, surrounding himself with an entourage of dancing masters, composers, poets and other leaders in the arts. These artists developed new musical compositions and elaborate performances for Louis and his courtiers. Even before Louis consolidated his reputation as ruler of the universe, turnout of the legs was regarded as an emblem of aristocracy and male beauty. Turnout, usually at 45°, showed the male calf to advantage while drawing attention to courtiers' elegant footwear. In 1661, as his own dancing declined, Louis founded the Royal Academy of Dance as the world's first ballet school, later to become the Paris Opera Ballet School. With ambitious ballet masters exerting total control over children selected from the poorest and hence most vulnerable citizens, ballet technique became ever more demanding.

In 1830, the renowned dance teacher Carlo Blasis wrote the first manual of ballet technique: *The Code of Terpsichore* (Blasis, 1830). Blasis' approach to ballet as a classical art form appears to have been a combination of the mathematical precision of classical Roman architecture seen in France's *Maison Carrée* (16BC) and in the organic fluidity of the Greek sculpture *The Winged Victory of Samathrace* (ca 190BC). Blasis' own drawings show his emphasis on mathematical precision in 90° turnout of each leg and foot, with the gesture leg being placed precisely at right angles to the pelvis. Although anatomically impossible, these requirements became the accepted goals for ballet teaching, leading to almost two centuries of hip, knee and spine damage. Today, most teachers have a basic

*Figure 4.1* The Maison Carrée, a Roman temple built in 2AD in Nîmes, France.
*Source*: Roly-sisaphus is licensed under CC BY-SA 2.0.

understanding of human anatomy but, for some, a subliminal desire for their students to produce 'perfect' positions prompts them to ignore reality.

> For dancers, particularly young dancers, striving to attain impossible goals can lead to physical and psychological harm. Classical ideals aim for beauty of the mind as well as the body, with the intention of bringing the viewer intense aesthetic pleasure and intellectual satisfaction.

From the first, classical ideals were believed to produce beauty, a highly desired virtue. Romantic ballets, created as classical technique was evolving, did prioritise beauty for the senses, often echoing Romantic themes of love and betrayal. The choreography was simple and harmonious, as appropriate for the equally simple stories. At the time, Romantic ballets revelled in the spirit world, with beautiful wraiths and vindictive witches eager to interfere in the lives of mortals. Their emphasis on airy lightness led a Danish choreographer, August Bournonville, to create a new training method and style of dancing – still Romantic but focused on effortless *ballon* (jump bounciness) and nimble footwork.

32  *Unveiling dancers' artistry*

*Figure 4.2* The 'Victory of Samothrace', sculpted around 190BC in Samothrace.
*Source*: Public domain, via Wikimedia Commons.

*Figure 4.3* An arabesque drawn by Carlo Blasis for his 1830 teaching manual, *The Code of Terpsichore*.
Source: Public domain (Published 1830).

Bournonville's joyous technique and style still delight today's audiences in the Royal Danish Ballet's performances of *La Sylphide* (1836) and *Napoli* (1842). As the Romantic era declined, Marius Petipa and Pyotr Ilyich Tchaikovsky launched an explosion of ballets underpinned by classical principles of balance and harmony, crowning their extensive repertoire with *The Sleeping Beauty* (1890) and *Swan Lake* (1895). These ballets, with their more complex choreography, greater technical challenge and slightly more nuanced characters, epitomised classicism in ballet, and they are still regarded by many as the embodiment of beauty in dance. In the eyes of others, ballet was a relic of the past.

By the beginning of the 20th century, a host of dancers across Europe and the United States reacted to the 'unnaturalness' of ballet's formal technique. To emphasise her

34  *Unveiling dancers' artistry*

*Figure 4.4* Isadora Duncan dancing in a garden.

*Source*: Photographer: Arnold Genthe. Public domain, via Wikimedia Commons.

opposition to ballet, Isadora Duncan (1877–1927) shocked the world by revealing the full beauty of the natural dancing body while wreathed only in floating scarves. Duncan's and other dancers' rejection of ballet technique triggered an explosion of expressionist and modern dance. Eventually, Martha Graham, an American modern dancer, created her own aesthetic and technique to facilitate the expression of extreme emotion. Paradoxically, Graham's technique places demands on the dancer's body that rival those of ballet technique.

Since then, many other contemporary dancers and choreographers have developed their own techniques according to their aesthetics and their beliefs about the body as an

*Figure 4.5* Martha Graham in in her solo, 'Lamentation'.
*Source*: Attribution 2.0 Generic (CC BY 2.0).

expressive instrument. Amid all these developments, the continued existence of ballet and its technique is remarkable.

Twentieth-century choreographers gradually broadened their subject matter and expressive range to encompass the full reality of human emotions and experiences. Ballets like Antony Tudor's *The Lilac Garden* (1936) were founded on classical technique, but they confronted audiences with contemporary psychological insight. In 1958, *The Diary of Anne Frank* inspired Kenneth MacMillan to create *The Burrow*. He moulded and extended ballet technique until it could express the horrors of human suffering in war. Throughout the 20th century, Tudor, MacMillan and countless other choreographers stretched the boundaries of the ballet aesthetic to speak as contemporary voices in their complex world. While psychological ballets may not always be beautiful in the conventional sense, it may be entirely possible that a finely crafted, creative, emotionally honest ballet that evokes new understanding in its audiences could be considered beautiful, regardless of its conventional prettiness. Over recent decades, classical ballet technique has been stretched far beyond that imagined by Blasis in 1830. Choreographers reflect and challenge contemporary aesthetics and, in doing so, they reveal the very bones of classical technique. With the present day's preference for streamlined clarity and purity, classical technique has never been more imaginative or more beautiful.

Despite ballet becoming ever more creative, expressive and experimental, it is interesting to note that increasing knowledge of anatomy and physiology has encouraged some teachers to focus on the developing dancer as a physical instrument. By controlling, stretching, and strengthening various components of the physical machine, then coordinating their interactions, the young dancer should be capable of amazing technical feats. In some cases, this mechanical mindset does produce technically outstanding students, but it is essential to bear in mind that dance, and ballet, are not only physical in nature. As Part 2 of this book shows, the mind and body cooperate with a complexity we could never emulate through conscious thought. Attempting to override natural processes with the aim of achieving perfection is not always appropriate in a creative, expressive art form. In fact, the expressive potential of movement can weaken when dancers aim for perfection. Ideally, the human body is constantly adjusting, from minute variations in neural control, to variable muscle and joint control, to postural sway. This perpetual state of change gives vitality, or 'life', to the dancing body. Furthermore, Bernstein's research states that when a person repeats a movement, the repetitions are never identical (Bernstein, 1967). *Perfect* is defined in the Cambridge Dictionary as 'faultless, correct in every way'. However, the living body is in a constant state of variability, making it impossible to reproduce a specific position or movement previously judged as 'perfect'. Perfection is an unachievable, and therefore useless, goal in dance.

> *No one is ever perfect in ballet, but when you can feel present and free, no one can tell you that how you were in that moment was anything less than perfect.*

In contrast to ballet's focus on perfection, Todorov and Jordan (2002) and many other researchers propose that motor control aims to produce 'optimal' performance, or the best possible performance in the circumstances. Repeating a 'perfect' *arabesque* is an impossibility, but optimal *arabesques* (beautiful, expressive, efficient and safe) can be created time and time again.

Although they may have discarded perfection as a goal, ballet students hoping to gain professional contracts ask themselves many questions: What does it feel like to be a ballet dancer? Is it as glamorous as it looks? Is it as hard as people say? Will being a dancer fulfil my dreams and make me happy? Will I miss out on a 'normal life'? Certainly, professional dancers' daily lives are different from those of their non-dancing friends, but whether they are better or worse depends on individual preferences. A few fortunate dancers seem to have been blessed from early childhood with an instinctive understanding of their future role as professionals.

> *Right from an early age I had an instinct to arrange my movements in a certain way that would feel as pleasurable as possible. So when I was on stage, all I had to do was remember how I wanted to 'feel' in a particular movement or step, and that would guide me.*

As can be seen in Chapter 1, many of the dancers who contributed to this book have found joy and deep fulfilment through dancing. At best, they show growth through meeting the inevitable challenges of their careers. These dancers are on a constant journey, discovering how their emotions and creativity can illuminate the music, the theme and the movement. Their ongoing explorations are the equivalent of scientific research in other fields.

> *It used to be enough to just feel the music, perform with emotion and become the character – but I feel like now there needs to be more. That with more thought and*

*technical assuredness, that there can be more freedom, and technique can speak for itself. That is the current challenge!*

Possibly the most significant change in approach as dancers progress lies in the realisation that 'thinking', a process so much admired in students, should take a back seat.

*The best sensation is when your body, the movement and the music are 'driving,' whereas 'you' (your conscious, intellectual awareness) can sit back and enjoy the ride!*

The experience of 'enjoying the ride', which is related to flow, can be intoxicating.

*You are in a sort of zone where your body and your mind are one.*

However, regardless of their progress in artistic and technical terms, dancers face other challenges.

*I guess that's why ballet's revered so highly; because it is such a risk, there are no guarantees. You give up so much of your time and energy for something that might not work out the way you want it to. It's such a challenging art to get right in the timing of your rehearsals, how much you train, how much you rest, injury, casting changes, how much touring you are doing, what's happening outside ballet in your personal life, physically, emotionally, mentally, financially.*

Since dancers are heavily invested in developing their skills and improving their performance in circumstances that are not always predictable, they need to acquire coping mechanisms to sustain their mental and physical health throughout their careers. Over the past few decades, researchers have examined whether programs of sustained effort over time, such as sport, music or ballet training, influence the brain. One famous study involved London taxi drivers. To gain a London taxi licence, drivers had to undergo two or more years of rigorous training in 'The Knowledge' – an extensive mental map of London's 25,000 convoluted streets and associated traffic rules. This map enables them to navigate rapidly and efficiently around the city in any traffic conditions. Maguire and colleagues studied the effect of this enormous amount of spatial navigation memory on taxi drivers' brains (Maguire et al., 2000). When comparing results with those of people who did not drive taxis, the researchers found significantly greater volume in the drivers' brains' gray matter (which processes muscle control and sensory perception) in the areas storing spatial representation. This suggests that the taxi drivers' memories relied primarily on the physical shape of London's road plan and the sensory memory of navigating the streets rather than on street names.

'The brain is the source of behaviour, but in turn it is modified by the behaviours it produces. This dynamic loop between brain structure and brain function is at the root of the neural basis of cognition, learning and plasticity' (Zatorre et al., 2012). In other words, almost everything we do, think and remember changes the brain in some way, and most of these changes facilitate our performance. Our brain's plasticity (ability to change) is key to our learning from birth to old age. *Structural plasticity* refers to the changes in the brain's physical structure in response to learning and new memories, whereas *functional plasticity* refers to the brain's ability to adapt to the environment and to injury (Demarin et al., 2014).

Since dancers spend years acquiring movement-specific knowledge and skills, researchers have looked for any identifying changes in their brains. They found that highly trained dancers' brains are, in fact, different at both structural and functional levels. Expansive research by Burzynska and colleagues found differences in several areas involved in dance movement (Burzynska et al., 2017). Activation of the Mirror Neuron System (discussed more fully in Chapter 6) is stronger and more frequent in dancers, leading to stronger connections between relevant brain areas than in non-dancers. These researchers also found that some motor learning areas are connected differently with other brain regions in dancers. One area of noticeable variation is related to pirouettes and other quick turns. When non-dancers spin, their vestibular systems (the orientation and balance mechanisms in their inner ears) produce a sensation of vertigo or dizziness. In dancers, it appears that signals from the vestibular reflex become disconnected from visual signals. This finding is supported by evidence that dancers have less white matter (which relays signals between different regions of the brain) in the area processing vestibular function (Nigmatullina et al., 2013). The disconnection between vestibular and visual information may allow dancers' brains to rely on the apparently still images captured by their eyes during 'spotting' – keeping the eyes and head focused on one spot for as long as possible during the first half of the turn, then quickly flicking the head over the other shoulder so the eyes and head can focus back on the same spot for the rest of the turn. This may explain how spotting prevents dizziness in dancers.

Despite these interesting findings, Burzynska and colleagues reported that dance training is not related to differences in cognitive abilities such as fluid intelligence or processing speed, spatial working memory or switching between tasks (Burzynska et al., 2017). They also suggest that dance training does not necessarily transfer to other cognitive abilities. In fact, dancers were slightly slower than non-dancers in a spatial working memory task – an unexpected finding that the researchers suggest could be due to dancers using different strategies from those used by non-dancers.

In non-dancers, current engagement in activities requiring coordination, such as sport or fitness, was related to improvement in balance performance. Surprisingly, the same researchers found that dancers' balance performance did not appear to be related to their dance experience. Their findings suggest that the dancers might have reached the ceiling for their balance performance early in their training. Related research shows that, compared with non-dancers, expert modern dancers have increased density in certain areas that govern motor control and increased connectivity in other motor areas (Li et al., 2015).

Hänggi and his colleagues (2010) reported evidence of structural differences in dancers' brains, including additional cortical thickness (increased gray matter) in their sensorimotor areas, which govern movement. A later study comparing dancers and non-dancers found dancers had larger volumes of gray matter in areas related to complex movement memory, possibly because they are required to remember numerous complex movement combinations on a daily basis (Dordevic et al., 2018). On the other hand, they found significantly smaller volumes in areas controlling limb movements – a fact that could be related to ballet technique becoming increasingly automatic with training. Automatic skills are less reliant on the relevant white matter, so structural plasticity reduces the spare white matter to make way for new learning.

Christensen and colleagues revealed another difference in professional ballet dancers' and ballet students' brains when compared with the brains of non-dancers (Christensen et al., 2017). Interoception, which involves a conscious experience of signals from the body, including heart rate, temperature, arousal, hunger and itch, is regarded as playing a key role in consciousness and self-awareness (Tajadura-Jiménez & Tsakiris, 2014). As may be guessed, interoceptive accuracy refers to a person's accuracy in feeling interoceptive signals, and it is reported to be related to emotional sensitivity, altruistic behaviour, emotional resilience and possibly to emotional well-being. Interoceptive accuracy is measured by a participant's accuracy in feeling and reporting their own heartbeat. The Christensen research measured the interoceptive accuracy of participants with no dance experience (Controls), dancers with 8–17 years of dance experience (Junior dancers) and dancers with 18–30 years of dance experience (Senior dancers). The Junior dancers' interoceptive accuracy was significantly higher than that of the Control group, and the Senior dancers' interoceptive accuracy was significantly higher than that of the Junior dancers, indicating that years of dance experience increase interoceptive accuracy. Subsequent studies have also shown that ballet dancers have higher emotional intelligence than controls (Atamturk & Dincdolek, 2021; Kordahi & Hassmén, 2022).

Since differences have been identified between dancers' and non-dancers' brain structure and function, it may be interesting to consider whether dancers' minds also show differences related to dancing and dance training. While the brain is a physical structure, a tangible part of the body, it is more difficult to define the mind. The revered neuroscientist Antonio Damasio describes the mind as a 'movie-in-the-brain', private, hidden and observable only by the owner (Damasio, 2000). Psychological research reveals certain changes in some dancers' minds that can be ascribed to their training.

Professional ballet training involves constantly increasing performance demands, requiring 'physical effort, time, energy, concentration, focus, and commitment whilst going through a well-documented period of physical and emotional growth and development' (Carattini, 2020). Young dancers are required to cope with ever-increasing demands in dance training and academic schooling while managing the challenges of adolescence, often without the support of a family environment or external friendships. These expectations, far beyond what is considered normal, may be related to ballet students developing 'moderately high levels of psychological inflexibility' when compared with non-dancers (Serrano & Espirito-Santo, 2017). Psychological inflexibility has been defined as 'a pattern in which behaviour is excessively controlled by one's thoughts, feeling and other internal experiences' (Levin et al., 2014). Psychological inflexibility includes two aspects: cognitive fusion and experiential avoidance. The first, cognitive fusion, describes a situation where an individual's excessive focus on memories, thoughts, judgments and evaluations leads them to adjust their behaviour according to these experiences rather than to reality (García-Gómez et al., 2019).

> *Doubt sometimes takes over. If I have done a step well 27/30 [times] in rehearsal, I have the fear of those three times which went wrong and the possibility of it happening on stage. Torturing!*

The second aspect, experiential avoidance, is defined by the same researchers as a situation in which a person avoids thoughts, feelings, images and sensations they regard as negative. As a result, the person avoids potentially upsetting situations in the hope of temporarily decreasing the discomfort those events might cause (Hayes-Skelton & Eustis, 2020). Experiential avoidance has been shown to be significantly related to harmful features of perfectionism (Santanello & Gardner, 2006).

> *I didn't feel ready to graduate from my ballet training, especially as I was the only graduate that year. I felt like a fraud, that people would see that I wasn't 'good enough'. On the day of my graduation, I became sick – vomiting, diarrhoea – and I missed my*

*graduation performance. I realised years later that my believing I didn't deserve to graduate was behind it all.*

Carattini notes that ballet students who have not acquired healthy coping mechanisms 'can feel unsafe in their learning environment', wary of taking risks, making mistakes or speaking up in class. Their fear of losing face in front of the teacher or other students can prevent them from being their authentic, or true, selves (Carattini, 2020). On the positive and more practical side, Noh and colleagues (2003) showed that dancers who had received training in coping skills spent less time injured than those who had not. Considering the link between coping mechanisms and performance, psychological skills can be an invaluable aspect of a 'toolbox of strategies that could help students remain resilient in the face of challenges while training' (Carattini, 2020).

Mindfulness, which focuses on curiosity, openness and acceptance of the present moment, has been proposed as beneficial for dancers and others suffering from psychological instability. However, research suggests that ballet technique's rigorous rules, combined with the focus on one 'perfect' model of achievement, may require a new approach by those influencing the mindsets of students and dancers. Serrano and Espirito-Santo (2017) found that ballet students had higher levels of both cognitive fusion and experiential avoidance than music students, and longer ballet training was associated with higher levels of psychological inflexibility. The answer may lie in psychological skills training such as that proposed by Carattini and a reassessment of the narrow focus of advanced ballet training. Ballet students willingly 'give their all' to become technically amazing, expressive dancers. It is up to ballet teachers to create new environments and methodologies that will support students' psychological health as well as their artistic development. The principle 'First, do no harm' must be as high a priority for ballet teachers as it is for the medical profession. How we can use emerging knowledge to formulate a teaching philosophy and practice in line with this ideal is a fundamental aspect of Part 3.

# 5 Dealing with challenges

At its best, a dancing career offers intellectual and artistic stimulus, together with the profound pleasure of harmonising the physical, emotional and musical aspects of performance. However, an art form that offers so much can also offer challenges. Even though anxiety, pain and injury can range from minor inconveniences to major problems, many dancers instinctively fear all of them as career threats. Ideally, a dancer confronted with anxiety, pain and/or injury can learn to seek professional assistance, to follow advice and to develop knowledge and resilience as armour against a similar threat in the future. Unfortunately, anxiety and pain can also indicate serious, even career-ending, injury, and it is incredibly difficult for an anxious dancer in pain to achieve a balanced understanding of their situation and the possible prognosis. This chapter hopes to de-mystify the issues in general, in the hope of giving dancers a basic understanding of their experiences.

*Anxiety* has been defined by the American Psychiatric Association (2023) as 'a normal reaction to stress and can be beneficial in some situations. It can alert us to dangers and help us prepare and pay attention'. In other words, anxiety is designed to help you deal with challenges. Researchers emphasise that 'anxiety itself is not a problem', even though severe and uncontrolled anxiety can have a negative impact on health and performance (Burin & Osório, 2017). A dancer's experience of anxiety depends partly on their individual psychological makeup. Some people feel anxious much of the time because they see many situations as threats. Others feel anxious when faced with a seemingly threatening situation, but their anxiety fades when their perception of threat passes (Walker & Nordin-Bates, 2010). It has been suggested that ballet may attract personality types who are likely to experience anxiety (Bakker, 1991).

Dancers can experience somatic anxiety ('butterflies', dry mouth, shakiness) and/or cognitive anxiety (worries, over-thinking, images of failure). Many researchers report that, in general, performers regard a certain degree of somatic anxiety as beneficial – it helps them feel ready to perform and raises their adrenalin levels enough to improve their performance. Cognitive anxiety, on the other hand, is generally seen as unhelpful. Dancers may imagine missing pirouettes, falling over, forgetting the steps, and other frightening prospects. Kenny studied the relationship between singers' anxiety and perfectionism. She found that perfectionistic performers use a great deal of energy evaluating their performance and 'end up developing a cognitive rigidity about concepts of success, mistake or failure, often rating success as all or nothing' (Kenny, 2011). Dancers can show similar tendencies, rating their performance as a failure unless it meets their own rigid criteria for success. This mindset may lead to students being praised for having 'high standards'. With praise reinforcing their unforgiving approach, they may establish unreasonably demanding, even impossible goals, thus setting themselves up for a lifetime of frustration due to their perceived under-achievement.

Anxiety can be related to the way dancers first learn technical skills. Decades of research have examined the relative effectiveness of explicit and implicit learning in high-performance fields. Explicit learning mirrors the technique used in most ballet classes: the teacher explains the exercise verbally and physically, and sets out the rules the student must follow, while the student memorises these instructions and uses them to control their movement. Explicit learning is by nature a cognitive (thinking) process, producing verbal knowledge that is stored in the dancer's working memory. In time, with long practice, explicitly acquired skills may become automatic, but this is not assured. Unfortunately, explicitly learned skills are vulnerable to fatigue, cognitive pressure and especially to anxiety. Athletes, and presumably dancers, who rely on explicitly acquired skills frequently underperform under stress because their automatic processes are over-ridden by conscious interference from thinking. On the other hand, implicit learning, the process that enabled us to learn to speak, walk and feed ourselves, relies on metaphorical imagery and sensory feedback. When you decide to reach for a glass of water, sensory feedback tells you where it is (visual sense) and how hard to grip it (tactile sense), then your kinaesthetic sense tells you how to move it to your mouth and back to the table. Implicit learning is independent of cognitive processes, and so it is resilient against stress and, importantly, against anxiety.

Principal dancers in ballet companies have been shown to experience higher intensities of anxiety than corps de ballet dancers do (Walker & Nordin-Bates, 2010). This difference may be due to the increased challenges and responsibilities facing principal dancers, but it could also be related to the personal characteristics that drove those dancers to reach the top level. Even so, anxiety can affect dancers at all levels. For instance, promotion to a higher rank can cause anxiety. Social anxiety can add to the stress of more difficult roles and greater exposure to possible failure.

*My sense of comfort changed dramatically when I became a soloist, especially when under-rehearsed. If a role was technically difficult, my focus during the performance would switch from performing to the most recent technical 'corrections' I'd been given. I didn't like being a soloist – I was scared everyone was jealous and waiting for me to make a fool of myself.*

Some challenges come, not from within, but from those eager to push an exceptional dancer's natural talent as far as possible. Unfortunately, interfering with a dancer's finely tuned psychological and motor processes can rob them of the innate talent that was integral to their success.

*There was a time where I 'forgot' or 'lost' my intuitive ability to dance when I was under more pressure (i.e., Principal Ballerina Phase!). It was almost [like] the more I had learned, the more I lost, in a funny way. You understand at some point that you have to 'un-learn' to come back to a more natural state of movement.*

This natural state of movement is described in previous quotes from dancers, such as, 'You are in a sort of zone where your body and your mind are one'. These words describe implicit control, with no interference from the cognitive system. Well-meaning coaches and teachers can ask an intuitive dancer to over-ride their natural implicit control with explicit control, thereby interfering with the very foundation of the dancer's unique talent.

Robbed of their inner security, a dancer in this situation is likely to experience high anxiety. Chan (2011) investigated the relationship between performance anxiety and self-esteem in music students. Her results suggest that 'high levels of anxiety might be associated with low level of self-esteem', a conclusion supported by subsequent research. The transition from a sheltered home and training environment to the sophisticated adult world of a professional ballet company, especially a touring company, can be challenging for new dancers. For a young person brought up in an environment of strict control and moral certitude, where self-confidence is suspect ('don't get too big for your boots, don't get a big head'), the upheaval can undermine their self-esteem.

> *Not feeling prepared/deserving/good enough for the role. Being too soft/vulnerable (from a religious upbringing), and now amongst harsher ballet company members. I was scared of them and not sure it was a 'safe' or the 'right' environment for me.*

To cope with their inadequate self-esteem, insecure dancers often seek external validation, 'pretending to myself and my teachers that I am good'. Unfortunately, pretending 'I' am good is based on an underlying belief that the real 'me' is not good – a potentially damaging mindset. One's own 'goodness' is not related to technical or performance factors.

> *I was afraid – mostly of my teachers' harsh judgement, but also of disappointing them. I would disappoint myself mostly. I really wanted to be really good! I thought about applying the techniques I was being taught (being a 'good' girl), dancing the music, pretending I was really good.*

A few dancers who contributed to this book discuss the effect on their dancing of low self-esteem and anxiety resulting from childhood trauma.

> *It's incredibly hard to achieve a feeling of harmony when you lack a deep, implicit sense of safety, trust and fun in your body. An intense feeling of being unsafe, closed-off and unable to fully 'access' your body can arise spontaneously (and often overpoweringly) without an obvious external stimulus.*

Another offered an eloquent description of his struggle to create a secure foundation in their fractured, fragmented world.

> *For my years in training when I was suffering most from the trauma, it was like my body, or at least my sensation of it, was a Jenga tower that was always re-structuring. There was no consistent, calm sense of 'being' underpinning my existence – let alone my dancing. I looked at dancing as this elusive thing I was always trying to manage and control and understand intellectually, because my body had no capacity to do so.*

For dancers suffering or recovering from trauma, the security of other dancers is unimaginable.

> *I remember looking at other people just step into 5th (position) – their bodies naturally assuming the shape – and thinking, how did they do that? I had to negotiate my body into every shape because it so rarely felt safe and relaxed.*

One of these dancers notes the impact of the studio environment on those who struggle to find a sense of security.

> *I find environments where you feel you can't laugh or get things wrong really damaging, especially when you're young. If you have people expecting you (even if it's not conveyed explicitly) to operate like a machine, you'll dance like one – and probably break like one too.*

But even for these dancers, a sense of safety can offer them the support they need.

> *When you feel safe – not just in a superficial, intellectual way, but on a deeper level where your nervous system can relax, integrate its experiences and be fully present – you can have fun dancing. This is always when you do your best work.*

Some of the dancers quoted in this section have a history of severe trauma, and they have managed to hide this for many years. As they express, the resulting damage to their inner security made progress in ballet technique very difficult, and it is to their credit that they became successful professional dancers. However, they could not begin to realise their potential in dance, or in life, until they began clinical therapy. Therapy enabled them to understand their trauma, to share it with their most important others and to build a sense of self-worth.

Trauma can be experienced in the ballet studio as well as in school and in normal life circumstances. The remarks about not feeling able to laugh or to get things wrong, and being expected to operate like a machine, indicate an atmosphere that can be highly damaging to a traumatised student, but this atmosphere is counterproductive for any student. Teachers may interpret a traumatised student's behaviour as sullen or uncooperative, or even as a sign of incompetence, while the student is struggling to find a sense of equilibrium. Ballet teachers are not trained to give therapy to traumatised students and should never attempt to do so, but they are well-placed to sense when a student is struggling. If that happens, a teacher can help by speaking privately with the student, gently asking whether they might need to talk to someone. Teachers should ensure the student understands that ballet teachers are not qualified to give professional help, but they can offer a sympathetic ear. If the student wishes, teachers can recommend further help, possibly by giving them a trustworthy chat line number or website address. At times, it may be appropriate to suggest speaking to the parents, but teachers should be mindful that parents can be part of the problem, and the student may not want them to know they are confiding in a third person. A traumatised student may not be ready to take the next step for weeks, months or even years after they first verbalise their problem. Regardless of the path the student decides to take in the first instance, the teacher can help by keeping the line of communication open while guarding the privacy of the student's situation and avoiding any pressure to take the next step. Above all, the teacher must never try to 'fix' the problem. However, the teacher can support the student by discretely reducing unnecessary stresses associated with their dance training, fellow students or outside events.

Anxiety is often related to pain – the much-feared signal that all is not well with the dancer's body. Fortunately, recent research has given us a much better insight into the nature of pain, its purpose and how it might be reduced or avoided. Like anxiety, pain is one of the ways your brain alerts you to possible danger, so pain may be defined as a conscious experience that urges us to protect our body. For example, if you burn your finger, certain heat-sensitive nerves in your finger send a 'Hey, unexpected heat sensation in the right index finger!' message to your brain. You do not experience pain at this stage. As an esteemed researcher says, 'No matter how large the mechanical, chemical, heat or cold stimulus occurring at the body, danger signals are not interpreted or felt as pain until the brain processes the incoming information' (Moseley, 2003). First, your brain considers the 'unexpected sensation' message in the light of previous experiences. It may decide the unexpected heat sensation is not dangerous and can be ignored, so you will not experience pain in your finger. However, if your brain decides the unexpected sensation indicates danger and protective action is necessary, it produces further nerve signals that make you feel a burning pain in your finger. As a result, you remove your finger from danger. Although this process protects the body, it is not fool proof. Determined dancers can convince their brains that certain 'unexpected sensation' messages are harmless, even when they are reporting real tissue damage. Also, the brain can continue reacting to old signals from a healed injury site, sending pain where protection is no longer needed. In some cases, the brain can produce 'phantom pain' sensations in areas that no longer exist, such as in an amputated leg. There have also been rare instances of individuals experiencing pain in a limb that was missing at birth, so it had never existed (Flor, 2002).

The emotional aspect of pain is now recognised as a crucial element in the pain experience, leading to a new definition of pain as 'an unpleasant sensory and emotional experience' (Bellan et al., 2017). Both physical and emotional circumstances influence our reaction to pain, and the experience of pain can be heightened or diminished by sensory (touch, sight, hearing, smell and somatic) stimuli. Fascinating research by Moseley and Arntz showed that illuminating a blue or red light while delivering an unpleasantly cold stimulus could transform the sensation from uncomfortably cold to painfully hot (Moseley & Arntz, 2007). Stanton and colleagues applied light force to the backs of patients suffering from back pain and spine stiffness, accompanying some trials with no sound, and others with the sound of a creaky door (Stanton et al., 2017). Results showed that participants over-estimated the force applied by the researchers in the 'creaky door' condition compared with the 'no sound' condition. In other words, the experience of pain can be influenced by unrelated factors. A dancer's pain can increase when the piano is out of tune, or when a certain teacher enters the studio to take class. The thought of putting pointe shoes on an infected soft corn can set up an orchestra of pain even before the shoes are out of the bag. Conversely, the euphoria of performing can supersede any pain, even when serious injury occurs mid-performance.

> *During a performance another dancer had to push me away in a fit of anger, but he accidentally thumped his elbow down hard on my face. At the end of the scene, the stage manager pointed out blood running down my face from an open cut on my eyebrow. I hadn't felt any pain because I had accepted the thump as part of the roles we were playing. The pain definitely came later though.*

Fear influences pain by motivating defensive responses such as fighting. On the other hand, anxiety responds to pain situations by activating a state of hyper-vigilance (extreme sensitivity to threat) and passive defensive responses like hiding or running away to protect the injured part. Positive emotional states usually reduce pain, possibly by reducing distress (Lumley et al., 2011). The purpose of pain is to make you stop contact with the painful stimulus and so prevent further injury. Ideally, anyone who feels pain from an object in their shoe, a knock or a stumble, will remove the cause as soon as possible. Unfortunately, the most common culprit in dancers is faulty technique over a long period, and dancers are not always prepared to, or may not know how to, improve their technique to remove the cause. Since pain is also an emotional experience, anxious dancers may see any pain as an indicator of serious injury and a threat to their performing careers – an overwhelming catastrophe for most dancers. Therefore, their sensitivity to physical pain is no doubt increased by their emotional response to that threat. Unfortunately, these dancers are inclined to turn their minds away from the feared outcome by pushing through pain, often with permanent consequences.

*I was in a hurry to dance – to grab the experience in both hands. I couldn't waste time trying to correct technical faults that were causing me pain. Actually, my hurry may shorten my career.*

Films like *The Red Shoes* and *Black Swan* and various books have promoted the idea of dancers as long-suffering martyrs, with pain and blood as emblems of their suffering. The general media have been happy to support this news-worthy stereotype, suggesting dancers spend their dancing days in agony and their retirement with deformed limbs and bodies. Historically, there is some truth behind these images. Not long ago, some ballet teachers still believed the outmoded 'no pain, no gain' mantra and encouraged students to push far beyond their pain threshold in the hope of overcoming physical limitations. Although bruised and bleeding toes can be controlled to some extent with new preventative measures, they are still a fact of life for those undertaking *pointe* work. Some students and dancers do undertake unhealthy practices to achieve unwise goals, and psychological problems can be found in both groups. These issues and attitudes can, and must, be addressed through education for all concerned, dancers, students, teachers, the public and the media. Each of us can help.

These days, some professional training institutions offer students comprehensive education in injury prevention and rehabilitation, alongside education in psychological skills that will support them throughout their careers. Some companies offer strong injury-prevention programs and rehabilitation support, but this is not the norm. In countries that do not provide subsidised health care, dancers may not be able to afford treatment for injuries or mental problems and may not be able to access outside clinics within their busy schedules. Dancers who can only rely on themselves are inclined to make decisions based on emotion and anxiety, rather than on the signals coming from their bodies and what these signals may mean for their careers in the long term.

*When I was younger, I would work through the tiredness, forcing my body with frustration, pushing my turnout, my physical state, which led to higher levels of pain and frequent injury. There was a refusal to listen to my body and myself, willing and forcing it to push through the tiredness and discomfort. It was as though I had pleasure in forcing and pushing past my limits. It was almost like an expression of angst – I wanted to dance things I wasn't dancing, I wanted to be doing things that I wasn't, rather than focusing on what my actual tasks were and where I was physically and emotionally in that current moment. I am (or I hope I am) past that point and realise that approach was extremely self-destructive and greatly reduced my performance capabilities.*

Praise for this sort of fanatical 'dedication' in students and young dancers only leads to frustration and self-blame when it hampers their training and careers. Unfortunately, the 'no pain, no gain' adage is still popular, despite abundant scientific proof of the physical and psychological damage it can do. Students can regard pain as a signal from their bodies that they are trying their best, proof of their willingness to do everything necessary to achieve their goals – confirmation of their romantic role as 'dedicated', as 'martyrs' to their art. Teachers sometimes praise students who sweat, tremble and grimace as they force their bodies beyond capacity, thereby establishing an unhealthy relationship between pain and praise. Without the teacher's intervention, these students are likely to suffer long-term physical damage and gain a warped understanding of the relationship between their bodies and ballet technique. Effective ballet training is designed to stress the physical body in carefully calculated, small doses so it will strengthen and adapt, enabling it to meet progressively more demanding challenges without causing damage. Students who are attuned to sensory feedback can assess and monitor the degree of stress that will be beneficial in any circumstance. For others, unhealthy attitudes towards pain can continue into a ballet career. A well-established dancer speaks regretfully of the long-term neural, physical and emotional effects of ignoring their body's signals over the years.

*Pain. Not much more to say there. Pain is the ultimate distractor. I should not perform or work with pain, but I did for so long, I have a hard time recognising the lines between pain and discomfort. (Which I am currently recognising as a very valid sign for me to stop dancing professionally).*

Female dancers in classical ballet companies can suffer sore feet from constant pointe work. Pain due to blisters, bruises, skin abrasions, toenail problems, cramps and muscle soreness is debilitating in itself, but young dancers who do not feel confident in their positions in the company can see their pain as shameful – a sign they are not good enough. These dancers often suffer in silence, adapting their technique to lessen the pressure and thereby risking permanent damage elsewhere in their bodies.

*The pain of my feet in pointe shoes – especially during or after long rehearsals. Especially if I had been sweating and didn't have a change of shoes or tights, so I was dancing in them wet – the whole bleeding feet thing was real for me and for many others.*

As can be seen in the previous section, anxiety can overwhelm a dancer's sense of control. The self-perpetuating cycle of anxiety, insecurity and fear predisposes dancers to injury.

*The biggest problem I find is fear and insecurity. When I am too nervous, I can't relax and let my body do what it needs to do, I overthink and over-correct, and this can often make things worse. Similarly, when I feel insecure and embarrassed about my ability as an artist, I become negatively self-aware and hyper-critical. This distracts me from being present in my body, and I become taken over by the voice in my head that is micro-analysing everything I do.*

Several of the contributing dancers mention similar factors in underperformance and injury.

*Distractions, criticism, mindset, anxiety, tiredness, physical pain, fear, embarrassment, hunger.*

48  *Unveiling dancers' artistry*

However, the same passion that drove these dancers to push past reasonable limits to achieve their dreams can sometimes, with maturity, help them to reset their approach.

> *I cannot afford another major injury (more for my mind and motivation's sake), and attention to my emotional and energetic state is now of the utmost importance for my physical health.*

As obvious as it may seem, long and successful careers depend on dancers achieving harmony between their minds, bodies and emotions.

> *There are days when you might be stressed and tense, tired and lack focus and energy, or a lack of confidence perhaps, so over-thinking may creep in. Experiencing all these things is how you learn about yourself if you take notice and observe. Most of the time it just takes reflection and then to step back, let go and relax. The body usually knows what to do all along.*

The dancer quoted here shows an innate understanding of the body's own wisdom and its deep integration with the mind and emotions, but research into the relationship between mind and body has revealed a deeper insight into how we move, reasons we move as we do, and how we can manipulate and change our movement. Part 2 of this book describes this emerging knowledge. Some readers may wonder whether Part 2 would be too scientific or too academic to be relevant to the practicalities of dancing and teaching. In fact, topics such as balance mechanisms, joint freedom, learning approaches and feedback are directly relevant to dancing and teaching, and to understanding other areas of this book. To assist in understanding scientific terms, they are listed in the glossary, along with page numbers for full descriptions.

# Part 2
# The magical motor system

# 6 The science behind the scenes

Our human capacity to engage in highly skilled movement, from microsurgery to Olympic gymnastics, is part of an evolutionary development we share with other higher animals. We owe our movement skills and emotional expressivity to single-celled ancestors whose rudimentary nervous systems enabled them to move towards food and away from danger (LeDoux, 2012). As evolution progressed, animals acquired exceptional movement skills specific to their needs, from the sinuous fluidity of cats big and small to the soaring eagle's mastery to the spell-binding dexterity of various types of monkeys. Many of these higher animals can also express emotion – a head tilt, lift of eyebrows, pricked ears, rapt attention or cowering in fear. As humans, we too have movement and expressive skills suited to our environment and needs, but dance requires an extension of these abilities. Dance devotes its capacity for skilled movement to expressing ideas and emotions, to creating new perceptions and to connecting with its audience in ways other means of communication cannot.

> *Emotional feeling is very important to me as an artist and is probably a very personal area. While it can be challenging to trust, or 'go there', that is the space where invaluable individuality and present-ness can be accessed. The aim is embodiment. This means, for me, a connection to the artistic parts of myself (as a person, a technician and as a character) and the objective I am trying to accomplish.*

Although dancers and ballet teachers can achieve success with no knowledge of how our brains and bodies collaborate in creating movement, a brief insight into motor control can help resolve dancers' technical difficulties when they arise and can reveal simple ways to enhance voluntary movement. Motor control can also offer dance teachers a broader understanding of the processes behind their students' learning.

The brain's first and most important responsibility is to keep the person alive and functioning. Its primary tool is the nervous system, which controls all body functions, including motor control and movement itself. Therefore, the motor system makes use of all the mechanisms discussed in Part 2 to optimise both performance and physical health. Motor control has been defined as 'the science of the nervous system's interaction with other body parts and the environment to produce purposeful, coordinated movements' (Latash, 2012). Russian researcher Dr Nikolai Bernstein (1896–1966), who is generally regarded as the father of motor control research, filmed several professional blacksmiths as they repeatedly struck a chisel with a hammer (Bernstein, 1967). He noted that the trajectory of each blacksmith's arm was slightly different in each of his strikes, thereby showing that the brain exploited a range of joint trajectories to ensure overall accuracy (Latash, 2012). Advances in medical imaging technology have enabled enormous progress in understanding this fascinating area, now known as motor variability. Although a few differing theories have arisen over the years, this book aims to present information that is widely accepted by most researchers.

> Motor control research presents many findings that are important to dancers and their teachers. These include links between variability and overuse injuries, and between degrees of freedom, flexibility and movement fluidity.

The nervous system is the network of nerves controlling most of the body's functions. It consists of the central nervous system and the peripheral nervous system and works in conjunction with the endocrine system. Nerves themselves are cordlike bundles of fibres acting as messengers, transferring information between the nervous system and other areas of the body. The central nervous system (CNS) consists of the brain and the spinal cord. The brain is a highly complex organ with overall responsibility for thought, speech, memory, emotion, sensory awareness and essential body regulation processes such as respiration, temperature and hunger. It is also responsible for planning movement, processing information from the senses and sending information to the body. The spinal cord acts as a messenger, carrying information between the brain and the muscles throughout the body to produce and refine movement. The peripheral nervous system (PNS) consists of nerves outside the brain and spinal cord. These nerves carry sensory information between the body and the CNS to help it control movement. The PNS can be divided into the somatic nervous system; the enteric nervous system, which controls the digestive system; and the autonomic nervous system, which regulates involuntary movements such as heartbeat, blood flow and breathing. Coordination between the CNS and PNS is essential to life. The third component of the nervous system is the endocrine system, which coordinates with the nervous system in responding to internal and external changes in the body, managing hormonal changes and maintaining equilibrium in the body's life systems.

*The best thing about performing is that it's harder for your intellectual mind to zero in on one thing more than another. You're forced to let your body drive. This comes with a feeling of being really present for each moment, and all the sensations/images/feelings of the performance move through you in an organic and expressive way. In short, you have the sensation of 'feeling everything all at once' onstage, but the sensation is integrated and energising.*

Dancing and all other voluntary movements are regulated by the sensorimotor system, which integrates all the sensory, motor and other elements required for interaction with the environment. Sensori refers to the senses, and motor refers to movement. The senses are nerve receptors recording information about the state of the body and its environment. The five senses have been well-known ever since the Greek philosopher Aristotle listed them more than two thousand years ago. Their early identification may be because their sensory organs, namely eyes, ears, nose, mouth and skin, are clearly visible. Aristotle's list is:

- Sight (vision);
- Hearing (audition);

- Smell (olfaction);
- Taste (gustation);
- Touch (tactual sense or haptic sense).

Somatic (body) senses register signals from receptors throughout the body. They play a crucial role in normal functioning and in movement control. Neurologists cite varying numbers of somatic senses according to how they classify them – a few neurologists name up to fifty-three senses! For dancers, the most important somatic senses may be:

- Proprioception (joint position);
- Kinaesthesia (motion through space);
- Vestibular system (balance and spatial orientation).

The brain's motor cortex oversees planning, controlling and producing voluntary movements, from getting out of bed, to showering, to grand allegro. An increasing number of motor-control research studies has led to a range of theories about the initiation of a voluntary movement. At this time, extensive brain scans before and during subjects' movement have led to a view that the brain starts laying the groundwork for a voluntary movement before the person is conscious of their decision to move. Haggard compares this situation with having a 'prior intention' to telephone a friend at some time, then an 'intention in action' when actually making the call (Haggard, 2005). As soon as the prior intention is formed, the motor cortex creates a motor plan, also known as a motor program, which coordinates the movement. Rather than plan each movement from a blank slate, the motor cortex searches the brain for previous plans with similar goals and uses the closest match as a basic template to formulate an intention-specific motor plan. As soon as the motor cortex creates the new motor plan, it also creates a predictive model that estimates the plan's effect and compares it with the original intention. If necessary, the motor cortex adapts details of the predictive model to ensure efficient performance. Refinements to the motor plan made in response to feedback from the predictive model are extremely quick. To activate the updated plan, the motor system sends electrical signals down the spinal cord to the muscles.

As soon as the movement begins, the sensory system sends a separate stream of feedback to the motor system so it can ensure the movement is as efficient and as close to the predictive model as possible. If sensory feedback shows any deviation from the prediction, the motor system automatically adjusts the muscle activity. However, these late-stage refinements are slower and less efficient than those made at the predictive model level before the motor plan is activated. This two-layered continuous feedback system, which usually occurs without our awareness, produces the best possible, or optimal, movement. Any additional feedback from verbal instruction or from looking at an image in the mirror occurs much later again. Since both verbal and visual feedback suggest changes to a motor program that is already under way, they are much less likely to lead to optimal movement. These findings support the view that information delivered while a dancer is moving will not be helpful.

Muscles only have two actions. They can contract, allowing them to pull two bones closer to each other, or they can stop contracting, either abruptly or slowly. Muscles cannot lengthen by themselves, so they work in pairs or groups. If the biceps (the big muscle on the inside of your upper arm) contracts, it pulls your lower arm to your upper arm, thereby bending your elbow. To straighten your elbow voluntarily, you must contract your triceps (on the outside of your upper arm). The biceps can improve control by gently resisting the triceps, or it can relax and leave the movement uncontrolled. When a muscle is contracting to cause a movement, it is called the 'agonist', while the opposing muscle is called the 'antagonist'. When the muscles swap their agonist and antagonist actions, the movement reverses. Fine coordination between our muscles' agonistic and antagonistic actions is a hallmark of excellent motor control.

While motor control in general receives vast amounts of research, movement inhibition has received relatively little attention. Non-selective inhibition has been defined as voluntary cessation of movement that has already been initiated, like coming to a sudden stop at a red light (Coxon et al., 2007). On the other hand, selective inhibition refers to the ability to stop one aspect of a movement while continuing with another aspect, as in pausing a head movement while continuing a *port de bras*. These researchers found that selective inhibition is a more difficult task for the motor system than non-selective inhibition. In both cases, the brain's motor system is pre-occupied with controlling the movement in progress, so any inhibition must be managed by cognitive motor control, or conscious effort. Even movement suppression, or keeping a part or parts of the body still, is known to be challenging for the motor system, as it requires control of the suppressive actions and also the stability of nearby body parts (Carpenter & Noorani, 2017).

> From the dancer's point of view, one of the most relevant features of the motor cortex is its plasticity, or ability to change. The relationship between neurons and muscles can change with experience. This change can occur within just a few minutes. In other words, practicing a dance movement correctly for a few minutes may actually change your brain (Karin et al., 2016).

The central nervous system employs two tools for managing the incredible complexities of controlling voluntary movement: variability and degrees of freedom. Each time we repeat a voluntary movement, small aspects differ, even though the differences may not be visible to the observer. Developing his theories from his blacksmith study, Bernstein described this aspect of voluntary movement resulting from non-repetitive differences in neural and motor patterns as 'repetition without repetition'. These differences are known collectively as 'variability'. Neural variability occurs in the brain's neural processes because the brain activates many more neurons and creates many more neural responses than are necessary to carry out a specific task. One theory emerging from ongoing research is that the brain activates a large number of neurons so it can select a strategy that might achieve the goal most efficiently (Faisal et al., 2008).

> *If I performed a certain step well in one performance, I used to try hard to do it exactly the same way the next night. It never worked. For me, it is better to approach the step as if each time is the first time – [to] more or less invent it on the spot.*

Motor variability leads to slightly different activation of muscle fibres and the muscles themselves each time the movement is executed. Variability can also be measured between the movements themselves – the knee could be very slightly lower in the second attempt – but the differences are almost always too small to be seen. Researchers propose that this over-supply of acceptable options enables successful movement despite any unforeseen changes in conditions. Furthermore, 'there are many possible strategies to achieve a goal, and each might have a different associated cost (error, energy or time)' (Faisal et al., 2008). The brain places a high priority on minimising 'cost' by balancing the demands of avoiding error, saving time and conserving energy. The brain's processes and the body's autonomic functions use a great deal of energy, quite apart from the energy required for voluntary movement, so giving priority to any one factor would inevitably require a reduction in the others. Lisberger and Medina suggested that variability facilitates optimal but not perfect performance because the additional demands on neural resources, reaction times and energy availability required to achieve a perfect outcome would require humans to have bigger brains (Lisberger & Medina, 2015). Research of relevance to dancers links low movement variability with increased risk of overuse injuries (Nordin & Dufek, 2019). Excessive muscle tension is likely to reduce movement variability.

Low variability has been found to indicate an unhealthy state, while high variability is healthier (Hamill et al., 2012). However, exceptionally high variability can lead to poorly controlled movement and hence to injury. Variability can be equated with movement exploration and, as such, it is an essential part of motor learning. To facilitate the learning of new skills, the motor system increases variability. However, the motor system also relies on several other factors to ensure optimal movement and each, like variability, negates the idea of a single model of perfect movement.

From a basic structural point of view, the human skeleton is articulated by approximately two hundred thirty movable joints. For example, the arm has joints between the bones of the shoulder, upper arm, forearm, wrist, hand and each segment of each finger and the thumb. The spine also consists of joints between movable segments. The range of movement in a joint can be described by its degrees of freedom. The last finger joint can only flex or extend, so it has one degree of freedom. The elbow can flex or extend and pronate or supinate the forearm (turn the forearm to face upwards or downwards), so it has two degrees of freedom. The hip joint can flex or extend, rotate internally or externally, and abduct or adduct (move the leg sideways, away from or towards the body), so it has three degrees of freedom. From the perspective of motor control, this may seem a relatively simple set of possibilities, but few movements are confined to one joint alone. Leaning over to tie your shoelaces might involve several joints in your shoulders and spine, and in your hips to compensate for the change of balance. Tying your laces would probably involve most of your finger and thumb joints as well as those of your wrists and elbows. This and most other daily tasks present the brain with an overwhelming number of movement possibilities and joint actions, and hence the need to manage a great number of potential degrees of freedom.

When someone learns a new skill, the usual tendency is to reduce the task's complexity by locking one or more joints, thereby consciously or unconsciously 'freezing' some of the degrees of freedom (Gray, 2020). Freezing involves co-contraction (simultaneous contraction) of opposing muscles to prevent a specific movement in, or to lock, an aspect of a joint's range of movement. However, muscle co-contraction consumes additional energy and reduces coordination between the body parts that are essential to achieving ease of movement and performance expertise. Bernstein states that we control the degrees of freedom differently according to the stage of learning (Bernstein, 1967). In the early stages, a learner is likely to try to control a movement by freezing one or more degrees of freedom in one or two joints, and they may also freeze a few more adjacent joints, so they become one unit (Guimarães et al., 2020). Bernstein also proposed that we usually begin by freezing the distal joints (furthest from the centre of the body), gradually freezing more proximal joints (nearer the centre) if necessary (Bernstein, 1967).

> *Balance was always my weak spot. My ankles are very flexible, so I used to grip all the muscles in my ankles and feet. That made things worse. Now I think about energy pouring from my centre, down my leg and through the floor, and that definitely works better.*

In *adage* and other movements demanding good balance, students often freeze the joints in their hands and lock their hip and ankle joints in the hope of improving balance. Some even curl their toes in an attempt to grip the floor. In fact, freezing any of those joints prevents postural sway – the body's automatic balancing system. Even when unnecessary freezing enables something approximating an intended movement, the body usually appears stiff and inflexible. As skill develops, the motor system should gradually unfreeze any unnecessarily restricted degrees of freedom. Mastery is achieved when the motor system has learned to exploit and control the degrees of freedom so they can produce efficient, flexible performance in various circumstances. Ideally, degrees of freedom are controlled by the motor system, so the relative influence of explicit and implicit learning on the extent to which degrees of freedom are frozen and freed (Gray, 2020) is unlikely to be surprising.

> A basic understanding of the concepts of degrees of freedom and variability may encourage students to rely on their bodies' innate abilities and so avoid unnecessary tension.

Almost every movement disturbs the body's equilibrium (balance) and requires an unconscious adjustment of weight. Immediately before an intended movement is initiated, the motor planner programs an 'anticipatory postural adjustment' (APA). If you stand on two feet and wish to lift your left leg, an automatic APA will briefly transfer additional weight onto your left leg so it can push your body's centre of balance (centre of mass) onto your right leg. If you move your head, an arm or part of your torso in any direction, an APA will adjust your weight placement immediately before the movement to ensure balance. Although it can be extremely difficult to see or feel APAs, normal movement would be impossible without them. APAs are highly relevant to dancers, who may try to lock themselves in 1st or 5th position, with the weight evenly on both feet, before moving one foot in a *battement* or *retiré*. In fact, this strategy is useless – the motor system will not allow the working leg to move while it is still bearing half the body's weight. The motor system places a high priority on your physical safety.

The human body is not a stable structure. Given that its height is much greater than its base, that there are many degrees of freedom in the spine and other weightbearing joints, and that the whole structure is topped with a heavy, unstable head, it would seem impossible for humans to balance on two feet, let alone one, or on *pointe*. Nevertheless, they do. Intriguingly, the key to our apparent stability is our instability, exploited by the motor system in a strategy known as 'postural sway'.

> *It took me a long time to embrace postural sway. Muscle tension resulting from my fight to maintain balance actually prevented my innate balance system from operating.*

*Even when I understood the concept, I felt guilty if I didn't 'try hard' which, for me, meant tensing up.*

Postural sway, our primary balance mechanism, does not try to keep the body in a balanced position. Rather, it exploits the act of falling. If the body sways too far forwards, for example, the muscles along the back of the torso and legs will become lengthened, and reflexes within those muscles will trigger corrective actions. If another person or an object pushes someone's body into the same off-balance position, the same corrective actions will be triggered. However, if a person voluntarily moves into an identical off-balance position, the motor system classifies the displacement as an intended action, so the reflexes will not be activated, and corrective actions will not occur.

> From a dancer's point of view, locking any of the postural muscles to maintain balance will de-activate the body's reflexes and automatic corrective actions. This will interfere with postural sway, making balance less stable and reducing movement fluency.

At this point, it may be wise to clarify terms often used when discussing balance. The body's centre of mass (COM) is the point where the whole body's mass, or weight, is equally balanced in all directions. Theoretically, the body could rotate easily in any direction around that central point. The COM is usually situated just below the navel and midway between front and back, with its exact position depending on each person's physique. On the other hand, the centre of pressure (COP) refers to the pressure of any weight-bearing parts of the body on the supporting surface. The COP lies within the area supporting the person's weight. If a person stands evenly on two feet, the COP will be midway between the two feet. Lifting one leg will move the COP to the other leg (by using an APA, of course).

In addition to these stabilising mechanisms, the motor system coordinates the activity of two different types of muscles – deep muscles and global muscles. Deep muscles, also known as stabilising muscles or stabilisers, maintain stability of our joints – without them, we would collapse on the floor like stringless marionettes. Deep muscles are small and close to the joints, so they are extremely energy efficient – a necessary attribute when they must constantly maintain our stability unless our bodies are completely supported. Although the deep stabilising muscles are not under our conscious control, the motor system ensures they are ready to support any activity of the global muscles, thereby enabling well-coordinated movement.

Global muscles are also known as superficial muscles because they are nearer the surface of our bodies, or movers, because they move our bones. They include our biceps, quadriceps, hamstrings, gluteal muscles and calves, in fact almost all the muscles you can feel with your hands. They are larger and more powerful than the stabilisers, so they use a great deal of energy, and they tire quickly. Global muscles are under our conscious control (we can decide to contract our calves). Unfortunately for dancers, since conscious muscle control is incapable of activating all the relevant deep stabilisers, movement that relies on conscious control lacks the effortless grace that is fundamental to ballet.

The motor system relies on feedback from the sensory system to ensure movement is occurring as planned, especially when the movement is voluntary, as in ballet. Neural feedback is information sent between the sensorimotor system and the central nervous system. It is an essential aspect of skilled movement and of motor learning – in fact, neural feedback is essential for motor learning to take place. Without neural feedback, our *pliés* would never progress beyond our first attempt because our motor system would have no idea what we were doing. When we intend to move, our central nervous system (CNS) responds by sending the appropriate commands to our muscles. Commands from the CNS to the muscles are termed 'feed-forward', while responses from the body's and brain's networks back to the central nervous system are called 'feedback'.

> The most reliable and most useful forms of feedback come from the dancer's own sensory system. Learning to 'listen to', or be aware of, the sensations of your body's position and movement allows your sensorimotor system to improve your movement even before problems become visible.

All five external senses and the various somatic senses provide the motor system with continuous feedback on any movement's effectiveness and efficiency. Sensory feedback is always present, in everyday life and in class, rehearsal and performance. Sensory feedback enables the motor system to improve or finetune all movement, especially voluntary movement like dancing. Even when a dancer imagines performing a movement, the sensory system provides the relevant feedback, allowing the sensorimotor system to pinpoint potential problems and make any necessary adjustments before the movement is performed.

*Sensory and visual imagery are ingrained in my dancing – they allow me to do what would otherwise be beyond me.*

Most dancers are fully aware of the contribution made by their own visual information when they are dancing. Seeing the surroundings creates a point of reference, which helps the dancer to stay upright, to balance and to avoid obstacles, as well as providing a reference point for spotting when turning. Many dancers become strongly aware of the importance of visual feedback when performing pirouettes on a well-lit stage with the audience plunged into darkness, or when dancing in a powerful spotlight. Visual feedback can also be disturbed when being lifted or manipulated through unusual orientations, possibly head downwards, or being rotated above a partner's head. At times, the choreography calls for parts of the set itself to move, interfering with the dancer's sense of stability. Other culprits include masks, wigs, headdresses, hats, props, eyewear and many other destabilising requirements.

Since dancers want their movement to occur simultaneously with the music, music could be regarded as both a motivator and a partner rather than a source of feedback. However, other sounds contribute to a dancer's orientation. Subconsciously, we expect to hear the various sounds made by our contact with the floor or by other dancers. An abrupt bang when we expect a cushioned landing prompts the sensorimotor system to adjust our muscle control. Most female dancers are especially sensitive to any sound made by their pointe shoes, as it suggests inadequate skill or possibly poor pointe shoe preparation. The consequent embarrassment can cause the poor dancer to tense her muscles, restrict her movement and possibly hold her breath. Continuous loud noise levels and complete silence can both be disorienting. Of course, dancers are aware of the music, the stage manager's cues and, especially, applause.

Tactile (touch) feedback, especially from the floor, is another part of dancers' orientation system. Additional pressure on the big toe joint signals pronation or rolling inwards, ideally triggering a corrective action to establish effective alignment for weight-bearing. Continual large-scale weight shifts between the forefoot and heel, and between the inside and outside of the foot, are indicators that muscle tension may be interfering with postural sway. While tactile feedback should help activate automatic remedial actions, the body's signals from the eyes, muscles, joints and the vestibular system (the inner ear's balance system) are also designed to provide rapid feedback, possibly activating solutions to movement problems.

In contrast to feedback from the various senses, somatic awareness provides the dancer with an overall sense of their body. Somatic awareness was first identified by the philosopher Thomas Hanna in 1988. Hanna defined somatic awareness as 'looking at oneself from the inside out, where one is aware of feelings, movements and intentions, rather than looking objectively from the outside in' (Green, 2002). Somatic awareness means consciously experiencing the sensations of the body (the soma), including sensations of movement itself, including tension, ease or stiffness; of breathing; of balance; of the internal organs; and of emotion. Feedback from these somatic sensations helps dancers to develop their coordination and expressivity. Hanna's theories have been expanded in movement training systems such as Moshe Feldenkrais' *Awareness through Movement* and Frederick Matthias Alexander's *Alexander Technique*, and some ballet teachers incorporate somatic principles in their teaching.

> *I think it's challenging and confusing for the body to respond when thinking about individual muscles. Imagery, analogies, actions and use of energy are more creative ways to achieve a more synergistic movement quality, which is what dancers need.*

Another breakthrough in our understanding of motor control occurred in 1987. Researchers discovered that movement-related neurons in macaque monkeys were activated when they saw another monkey or a human perform a voluntary action such as picking up an object (Rizzolatti & Craighero, 2004). They called the activated areas of the monkey cortex 'mirror neurons'. Later, researchers discovered a similar but more complex process in humans and named it the 'Mirror Neuron System'. They found that the Mirror Neuron System is the only mechanism that 'allows an individual to understand the action of others "from the inside" and gives the observer a first-person grasp of the motor goals and intentions of other individuals' (Rizzolatti & Sinigaglia, 2010). Masterson's research demonstrates that the Mirror Neuron System 'acts as a pathway between cognitive processing and emotions, language and motor processing' (Masterson, 2015). Various research studies reveal that the Mirror Neuron System is responsible for observation, imitation and simulation of another person's movement and for understanding another person's intention. In other words, the Mirror Neuron System allows the observer to share in the other person's experience, to interpret their emotions and to feel empathy for their emotional state. The Mirror Neuron System is also involved in neural circuits for sensory perceptions, such as vision and touch (Bastiaansen et al., 2009). In addition, it is proposed as an element in 'theory of mind', which is the ability to understand other people's mental states as separate from one's own. Recent research has examined the role of the Mirror Neuron System in emotion regulation, language, music and motor processes, revealing its importance in wellbeing and healthy function. The Mirror Neuron System is sometimes known as the Action Observation Network.

> The Mirror Neuron System allows dancers to feel the unspoken meaning and emotions of their teacher, a choreographer and other dancers, while audience members' Mirror Neuron Systems allow them to share in the dancers' motivation and meaning during performances. Given the audience's insight into a dancer's internal experience, it is essential for dancers to focus on their artistic and creative goals rather than on technique or how much their feet hurt.

Most of these types of feedback rely on interaction between the brain's and body's innate processes for achieving goals, optimising movement and preserving physical health. However, humans also want to be able to produce movement that surpasses normal potential and to interact with a technological environment that was unimaginable decades ago. More importantly, for those of us in the dance world, we want our movement to communicate emotion, ideas and experiences, to speak the unspeakable, to express the inexpressible.

Sometimes, transcendent experiences are created in the interface of contemporary dance and classical ballet. In 1997, Carolyn Carlson, a contemporary dance choreographer, created *Signes*, a masterwork celebrating the symbiotic relationship between painting, music and dance. The artist Olivier Debré's series of powerful paintings, composer Réné Aubry's evocative score and the sublime dancers of the Paris Opera Ballet address all the senses simultaneously, arousing a cauldron of emotions, memories and the intellect.

# 7 Pathways to new skills

From birth, we learn to move in ever more complex ways so we can meet the challenges of daily life and all it may involve. The process of acquiring these skills is known as 'motor learning'. Motor learning has been defined as 'a set of processes associated with experience or practice which can lead to permanent changes in the ability to perform a skilled action' (Sharma et al., 2016).

Although dancers frequently perform choreography based on ballet technique, their words throughout this book show they want their movement to express their own emotions or those of the character they are portraying, to convey meaning and a sense of identity, to make music visible and to embody abstract sensations and concepts such as harmony or freedom. When considering motor learning in a dance context, Burzynska and colleagues stated that 'dance involves motor, cognitive, visuospatial, social, and emotional engagement' (Burzynska et al., 2017). For dancers, dance is not 'acting out' emotions, relationships and situations, but rather a direct communication received by the audience through their Mirror Neuron System. From the earliest ballet classes, ballet should be experienced as the expressive language it is, sowing the seeds for successful professional careers.

> *The music, emotional storytelling, and connection with another person on stage are all of great importance to me. They make me feel like there is a real purpose to what I am doing, and when those elements combine together, it allows me to go into another realm and become the artist who is creating the image and provoking the feeling I want the audience to feel. . . . I believe that is when a performance can really transcend the viewer.*

Our ability to learn new skills depends on our brain's 'plasticity' – its ability to change. Decades of research have shown that relevant brain areas increase in volume and thickness when a new skill is being acquired, presumably due to the increased number of neurons required to store new information gathered over repeated activation during practice. Neural expansion has been measured after a few sessions of balance training, after learning a foreign language, after studying for an exam, after mindfulness training and after several months of juggling training. Unsurprisingly, neuroplasticity also occurs when learning new dance skills. However, something perplexed early researchers: if the relevant areas of our brains increased in volume and thickness each time we acquired a new skill, our brains would soon outgrow our skulls. In fact, the expanded brain areas decrease as the skill becomes well-established, returning to near their previous volume without any loss of function (Wenger et al., 2017). Wenger proposes that this decrease is due to metabolic

DOI: 10.4324/9781003395188-10

efficiency – a pruning process that retains only the most stable and effective neural connections. Frequent use embeds the optimal set of connections, leaving a refreshable trace if the skill is not used for some time.

> It can be reassuring for dancers to know that their brains hold a trace of the most efficient and effective way of performing a skill they may not have attempted for months or even years. The brain can simply reactivate the previously perfected motor plan when necessary. The muscles may be out of practice, but the neural recipe for the skill is intact.

When discussing motor learning, it is important to differentiate between related concepts and to establish understanding of the way key terms are used in this book. *Cognition* refers to knowing or understanding something. Cambridge defines cognition as 'acquiring knowledge and understanding through thought, experience and the senses'. In her book, *The Human Condition*, philosopher Hannah Arendt describes the cognition process as finite – it aims to acquire specific knowledge and stops when it has acquired that knowledge (Arendt, 1958). She sees cognition as the basis of science. Thinking, or thought, is one component of cognition. Arendt says that thinking has no end point. She proposes that the human ability to think is the basis of the arts. Another aspect of cognition is learning, which involves the development or application of understanding or knowledge acquired through cognition, but it also contributes to further understanding and cognition. Cognition, however, is not the only way to achieve motor learning.

Imagination, an essential component of the arts, means being able to form an abstract thought or idea in your mind – it is a product of thinking. Imagery, by contrast, means creating a picture, sensation or image in your mind. Imagery is a product of the sensorimotor system. An image is defined in most dictionaries as a 'representation', so imagery can be a sensory representation in your mind of almost anything. Imagery was first studied in sport science with the aim of improving performance, so some terms reflect the needs of athletes and participants in sport. The acceptance of an image being a 'visual picture' or a 'visualisation' may serve sport well but that narrow, visually based concept is far from the rich sources of imagery used by dancers, including a physical shape, an experience like sinking or floating, a sensation such as wind, a sound, a picture, an emotion or something similar.

Sensing, or sensory experience, encompasses many senses: awareness of sensations such as smell and sight, sensing the floor with the feet and being aware of the rhythm of the music are all classified as sensory experiences. The somatic senses are more inclined to make themselves known to us when we are not well. Sensation of being physically unstable, cold, hungry, anxious, and nauseated are signals from our somatosensory system. This book follows Antonio Damasio's (2022) example by defining 'feelings' as the experience of emotions and their expression through the body rather than as a sensory experience.

> For dancers, all types of imagery can be valuable. Imagery can improve technical facility and can transform technique into artistry. Imagery helps dancers to express the full range of meaning and emotion to the audience.

Imagery conveys an idea or sensation to the sensorimotor system. Imagery affects the neural networks responsible for a movement, so the movement reflects the image's most relevant characteristics. For instance, imagery of a snake slithering into a crevice can imbue a movement with a snake's qualities (smooth, secretive, sinuous, seemingly boneless, sneaky, evasive or possibly dangerous) rather than the reality of the snake as a creature. Imagery is the language of the brain. Research into the effect of placebos and phantom limb pain indicates that the sensorimotor system does not distinguish between an actual situation and one's image or belief about the situation. Consequently, a person usually reacts or acts in accordance with their understanding of the situation.

The term sensory imagery usually refers to the five senses. Visual imagery may include colour, shape, pattern and events such as lightning flashes and darkening skies. It could also refer to representations of your own body, of another person's body, of an abstract body such as a marionette, of concrete or abstract shapes or of the environment. Frequently, visual imagery merges with other types of imagery. For instance, you could 'see' yourself as a wide-winged eagle while 'sensing' yourself gliding effortlessly, and 'feeling' yourself buoyed by rising currents of warm air (visual, kinaesthetic and sensory imagery).

Internal and external visual imagery are defined inconsistently among sports imagery researchers. According to Gaümann and colleagues, internal visual imagery (IVI) describes a first-person view, as if you are looking through a camera mounted on your own head (Gäumann et al., 2021). In this view, you would see your environment but only occasional glimpses of your own extremities. This could help players in open sports like football, golf and skiing, where players must interact with other players or with the environment. For example, football players retain images of game plans indicating how they should move among team members on the field. Dancers might use IVI to imagine their path among others on stage, or the way they and their partner move into a lift. Other researchers describe IVI as similar to a camera mounted inside one's own head, allowing the performer to scan their own body from the inside (Yu et al., 2016). Yu's description, being truly internal, seems closer to the way dancers use this form of imagery. External visual imagery (EVI) has differing definitions too. In Gaümann's view, EVI entails seeing your own movement from the perspective of a spectator, or as an image in a mirror or on television. On the other hand, Yu describes EVI as requiring 'an individual to visualize the movements generated by others in their surroundings, whilst the observer is a spectator'. Since it is not clear how an external spectator's perspective of other dancers would feed into a dancer's sensorimotor system or influence their movement, Gaümann's perspective on EVI seems to be more relevant to dancers. Pictorial or concrete visual imagery, which uses colours, objects and textures, may serve more often as a source of inspiration than as a link with the sensorimotor system. Although people often refer to visual imagery, the other senses can influence our movement in a more subliminal way.

Auditory imagery may include the sound of popping corn, of a waterfall or the ebb and flow of a musical phrase. Tactile imagery is based on the skin's sensation of touch, possibly of sandpaper, silk, running water, pinpricks or wind against the skin. Imagery of dancing under the hot sun, or in gentle rain, can transform an *enchaînment*. Olfactory imagery is based on sensations of smell – the heady, soporific scent of magnolias, the fresh sea air, a smouldering wood fire or bacon frying in a pan, while gustatory imagery is evoked by taste. Imagining your favourite smell is just behind your head can activate subtle changes in your head and spine alignment. Imagery of chocolate melting in the mouth, ultrastrong throat lozenges, sourness or bitterness can infuse shapes and movements with the unusual qualities. Despite the specific sources of the sensations, visual, auditory, tactile, olfactory and gustatory imagery are simply regarded as 'sensory imagery'.

> Dancers might imagine themselves as bouncing ping pong balls in *petit allegro* or moving through cream in *adage*.

*I generally find structured, concrete visual imagery to be distracting while in performance and prefer to rely on the other factors. I do think visually though, and so I do constantly have internal paint flows, shapes, and colours washing about – so those are constantly used when I am dancing.*

In contrast to sensory imagery, motor imagery is sometimes defined as practising movements in your mind without actually executing them, even though motor imagery also guides movement as it happens (Anema & Dijkerman, 2013). In fact, the term is an umbrella for many forms of imagery capable of influencing the way a movement is performed. Kinaesthetic imagery relates to the sensation of the body's movements, rather than its positions. The term kinaesthetic refers to the sensation or perception of movement. Kinetics is used more often in biomechanics to describe the forces that cause motion, and kinematics is used to describe motion. Although the terms kinaesthetic imagery and kinetic imagery are sometimes used interchangeably, kinaesthetic imagery is the term used in this book. Solodkin and colleagues examined brain patterns during visual imagery and kinaesthetic imagery and found that kinaesthetic imagery closely resembles actual performance 'by activating motor preparation, refining motor abilities, and initiating supportive physiological changes' (Solodkin et al., 2004). The researchers regard this as evidence that only kinaesthetic imagery is directly related to motor behaviour and can influence the preparation and the performance of a movement. Floating, falling, hovering, shivering, sliding, flying, shrinking or expanding – any of these kinaesthetic images can influence a dancer's movement quality. A *grand allegro enchainment* might be brought to life by imagining a large seabird taking flight, soaring and swooping.

Unlike these types of imagery, subjective imagery involves sensations generated within one's own body, such as fatigue, pain, hunger and thirst. Emotions like disgust and fear provoke subjective imagery, and some dancers use subjective imagery to convey strong emotions. Juliet may sense physical shock, inability to breathe and nausea as integral to her grief and despair on finding Romeo dead. Other dancers prefer to experience visceral emotions directly, by imagining their character's situation, rather than through subjective imagery. However, subjective imagery of cold, hunger, exhaustion and pain could be powerful in performances of *The Little Matchgirl* or the last act of *Manon*.

Metaphors allow us to present an idea through a statement that is not literally true. As an example, feeling fatigued could be expressed as 'I'm absolutely wiped out'. In motor imagery, the term 'metaphor' usually covers similes and analogies. Desai and colleagues (2011) scanned their subjects' brain activity during action sentences, abstract sentences and metaphorical imagery. Their results agreed with previous research that 'metaphoric action retains a link to sensory-motor systems involved in action performance'. This finding is highly relevant to dancers, as the imagery evoked by a metaphor can carry its meaning directly into the sensory-motor system and so directly influence the dancer's movement. Research also suggests metaphors containing verbs are more effective, possibly because verbs themselves are signals to the motor system. Metaphors can give life to an otherwise uninteresting instruction. Metaphors that are fresh, creative and sometimes funny are likely to be remembered. Metaphors with an emotional aspect are also persuasive. Since metaphorical imagery can have a strong and long-lasting effect on movement, it is essential to avoid the mocking, negative metaphors of the past. 'Is that your foot or a wet sock?' is as damaging to the poor dancer's motor control as it is to their self-esteem.

Mental practice is a different type of imagery. It involves performing an exercise or phrase in your mind, with the intention of reinforcing the knowledge you have gained in class or while watching others. Good mental practice also aims to increase coordination, remove unnecessary tension and improve phrasing. Mentally practising to music (real or imagined) allows you to colour your movement with dance quality and expressivity. Many dancers prefer to use mental practice in a quiet, calm environment, free from distraction and interruption. Even so, these conditions can be hard to find, and many dancers find some of their best 'aha moments' while strap-hanging on their way home from the studio or theatre.

*I find that visualization (mental practice) assists greatly in performance. Being able to see yourself performing exactly as you want to is, for me, the first step to successful performance, followed by finding the way it should feel.*

Mental rehearsal extends mental practice by placing the tasks within their environment. It is often recommended as a way to prepare for intimidating events such as examinations, auditions and concerts, where the surroundings for the event may be unfamiliar. We instinctively feel comfortable among familiar smells, sounds, temperature and places, so the stress of the unknown can be overwhelming. The idea of mental rehearsal is to map out and mentally rehearse the chain of events and experiences that will occur on the relevant day. Many people start their map from waking up (when, how), then morning rituals such as showering, dressing and breakfast. Keeping as close as possible to your normal routine keeps anxiety levels low.

Plan your travel to the venue, allowing additional time for traffic delays. As you imagine walking into the venue, sense your surroundings – the smells, the sounds, the light, the building itself. If you are not yet familiar with the venue, you may be able to visit it beforehand, or at least look at it from the outside. Feel as if this is your building, and the corridors, rooms and stage are your spaces. The next part of your plan involves all the details of preparation, class, make-up, costume, chatting with friends or maybe finding a quiet space. Make sure your plan allows for unforeseen circumstances such as a costume calamity, hair with a mind of its own or the casting being changed at the last minute. Finally, imagine yourself waiting in the wings and the excitement of going on stage to do what you have planned to do – dance. Now you are ready to put your mental plan in action. Your plan should be a framework, capable of adapting to circumstances while still arriving at a fulfilling performance experience. While many types of imagery can add richness and ease to dancers' performances, individual dancers may find one type or another to be more effective. The crucial point is that dancers can create imagery, and that is not always the case.

In general, and especially in artistic terms, 'phantasia' means the capacity to create imagery. Most research has focused on visual phantasia, describing it as 'seeing with the mind's eye'. However, phantasia also includes hearing with the mind's ear, smelling with the mind's nose, tasting with the mind's mouth and feeling with the mind's skin. Although different people experience differing degrees of vividness in specific types of imagery, the imagery section of this book will be more relevant to readers with some degree of phantasia. 'Hyperphantasia' refers to frequent experiences of exceptionally vivid imagery.

Hyperphantasia is frequently found in creative professions such as dance (Zeman et al., 2020). This research also revealed that people with hyperphantasia can be found among the most highly imaginative leaders in research and scientific creativity. At the other end of the spectrum, *aphantasia* is the inability to create mental images. Those with aphantasia are generally found working in computing, mathematics and science. They are more likely to have difficulty in remembering faces. *Synaesthesia* is a condition where a stimulus triggers more than one sense. As examples, a particular letter, number or word may always be accompanied by a certain colour or tactile sensation, whereas a specific sound may also be experienced as a taste or a smell (van Leeuwen et al., 2015). Those with hyperphantasia are more likely to experience synaesthesia (Zeman et al., 2020). All types of imagery can contribute to motor learning, but learning itself can occur in different ways.

Implicit learning describes the situation where we learn something even though we are unaware of learning it or how we learned it. Young children learn to grasp objects, walk and communicate through their native language, all without an instruction book or formal lessons. These are examples of implicit learning. Adults learn implicitly to control a computer mouse and to avoid bumping into new furniture. Implicit learners cannot explain how they learned the skill or acquired knowledge, because implicit learning is not the result of conscious thought, planning or instruction (Masters, 2008). Implicit motor learning in dance can be acquired through metaphorical imagery.

Implicit learning has many advantages. Skills acquired through implicit learning are better retained and remain effective under pressure and fatigue, such as in performance or competitions (Masters & Maxwell, 2008). Other researchers reported that 'implicit motor processes are stable under both psychological and physiological pressures' (Benson et al., 2011). Additionally, 'implicit motor learning results in performance that remains unaffected by concurrent cognitive demands, whereas explicit learning does not' (Masters et al., 2008). In fact, the implicit learning system does not seem to be limited in capacity (Dietrich, 2004).

Implicit learning can be achieved through 'trial and error', where learners are motivated initially by accidental successes. Through repeated attempts, they subconsciously reinforce the effective aspects of their attempts, while unhelpful aspects are ignored until they disappear. Since trial-and-error learning seems to be common to most sentient animals and can be seen clearly in human infants' early development, it may be the most deeply embedded method for achieving new motor learning. Another type of implicit learning is 'errorless learning'. Contrary to its name, errorless learning does include errors, but it attempts to keep them to a minimum (Poolton & Zachry, 2007). Errorless learning involves introducing a new skill in its simplest format, so it is easy to achieve with implicit control, before gradually increasing the task difficulty. Poolton and Zachry propose that errorless learning discourages declarative (explicit) knowledge and so increases resilience against fatigue and competing demands. With extended practice of an implicitly learned skill, the brain can create a 'mental representation', almost a hyperlink, to the details of the relevant motor plan. This mental representation is thought to be stored in long-term memory, thereby keeping it readily accessible to the motor system while saving the working memory's limited capacity. Unfortunately, mental representation, which occurs in the brain rather than the muscles, has become known by the misleading term of 'muscle memory' (Dietrich, 2004). Dietrich also proposed that the flow state, much enjoyed by dancers, is 'a period during which a highly practised skill that is represented in the implicit system's knowledge base is implemented without interference from the explicit system'.

In contrast to implicit learning, explicit learning is based on declarative knowledge and can be declared or expressed verbally. Explicit learning depends on factual knowledge, so it involves conscious thinking. In turn, conscious thought relies on working memory, which has a capacity limit of approximately four items at a time. According to Dietrich, 'explicit learning cannot occur if the rules governing the task reach a complexity that exceeds the capacity limit' (Dietrich, 2004). In dance, explicit motor learning usually relies on factual instruction from the teacher. If the instruction does not surpass the working memory's limit, a person who has learned a motor skill explicitly is able to describe how they achieve the skill. Traditionally, ballet teachers rely on explicit instruction, explaining details of body placement, limb articulation and muscle activation. Although this results in explicit learning and conscious control of movement, there is a possibility that these students' explicit knowledge might be transformed into implicit awareness over the long term. However, some students learn more quickly and easily by watching the teacher's movement and by creating images and sensations to facilitate their own learning. These implicit learners can become frustrated when asked to repeat factual knowledge, and teachers can become equally frustrated when the student struggles to repeat the teacher's explicit instruction. For these learners, conscious awareness of the 'nuts and bolts' of their movement interferes with their natural implicit control. Since implicit learning creates apparently effortless technique, it seems logical that implicit teaching should be the preferred option.

*When the teacher tells us how to do a step, how our bodies should move, I have to imagine how the movement should feel before I can do the step properly. When I know the feeling I want, the step is usually easy.*

Explicit learning stores the verbal instructions for a movement. When experts who initially acquired their skills through explicit learning are under pressure, they are at risk of 'reinvestment'. Reinvestment is the 'manipulation of conscious, explicit, rule based knowledge, by working memory, to control the mechanics of one's movements' (Masters & Maxwell, 2008). In simpler words, a person who is under pressure can revert to (reinvest in) rules and instructions acquired during explicit learning, thereby losing the advantages of implicit (automatic) control. Their previously automatic skills become forced as they try to recreate the way they learned them. Numerous studies involving surgeons, golfers, baseball batters, swimmers, trampoline performers, and soccer and football players have shown that reinvestment can severely compromise performance, resulting in an effect often known as 'choking' or 'getting the yips'. This condition, which is sometimes career-ending, can be avoided by learning skills implicitly and keeping verbal knowledge to a minimum. Teachers who feel frustrated by students' inability to recite verbal instructions can be reassured by knowing their students' knowledge is stored deep within their brains and is accessible to their motor systems whenever needed. For dancers, a crucial aspect of implicit cueing is that it focuses first on activating the deep stabilising muscles, thereby improving movement quality and stability.

Due to ongoing research, another approach to cueing movement has arisen. The focus of attention (FOA) approach utilises the concepts of implicit and explicit learning, but with a different method of cueing. When intending to make a movement, a person can focus their attention either internally or externally. With an internal FOA, a person focuses attention on the task's specifics – how their body will move, maybe including joint angles, muscle activity and coordination between body parts. Conversely, an external FOA places the person's attention on the effect of the movement, such as the path their extremities will follow or a target. An internal FOA may be compared in some respects to explicit learning, as both focus on the movement's mechanics, and both may be encouraged by teaching methods involving these details. An internal FOA for a *grand rond de jambe en l'air* may involve focus on the working leg's movement in the hip socket, turnout and the tilt of the pelvis. An internal FOA appears to face the same drawbacks as explicit learning. An external FOA is like implicit learning in many respects. In the *grand rond de jambe en l'air*, an external FOA might involve the working toes tracing a large semi-circle through the air. An implicit approach may go further, using imagery of a laser beam from the working side sit-bone, passing along the back of the leg and out through the toes to cut an enormous laser arc through the night sky. Importantly, this implicit cue seats the head of the femur (thigh bone) safely within the hip socket while directing the focus outwards. Also, the image of a laser passing through and beyond the leg encourages optimal balance between agonist and antagonist muscles.

An external FOA and implicit control both encourage the motor system to produce the desired result without conscious muscle activation. Poolton and Zachry (2007) used EMG to compare muscle activity while participants were focusing either internally or externally during a basketball free throw. When participants were using an external FOA, EMG readings showed less muscle activity than that of participants using an internal FOA (Poolton & Zachry, 2007). This and other studies suggest that an external FOA leads to more economical muscle activity, as implicit learning does. Others suggest that an internal FOA 'constrains the motor system by interfering with natural control processes, whereas an external focus seems to allow automatic control processes to regulate the movements' (Wulf & Prinz, 2001). An internal focus has been shown to produce higher EMG (more effort) in muscles required for a weightlifting task, but it also showed an increased activity in muscles not related to the task (Marchant & Greig, 2017). It has been suggested that the increased muscle activity may be caused by unconsciously freezing some degrees of freedom in order to control the movement, in contrast to the innate efficiency resulting from an external FOA or implicit learning (Poolton & Zachry, 2007). Subtle differences in instruction can encourage an internal or external FOA. As long ago as 1999, Wulf and colleagues asked players with no prior experience of golf to pay attention to their arm swing (internal focus) or to the club swing (external focus). Despite the arm and the club being relatively close in proximity, they reported that the external FOA group's results were 'impressive' in superior accuracy during the tests and also in retention tests one day later (Wulf et al., 1999). It is possible that focusing on the arc of the club head or even the desired trajectory of the ball may have yielded even better results.

Researchers suggest that instructional cues should be meaningful to the learner. While asking young students to point their toes to a certain number on an imaginary clock face will be more effective than asking them to lift their leg to 45°, cultural environments also play a part. To give a table tennis ball a topspin, a metaphor of a hitting the paddle up and over a right-angled triangle was successful with Western participants. However, participants in Hong Kong did not benefit from the metaphor until it was changed to 'Move the paddle as if it is traveling up the side of a mountain' (Poolton & Zachry, 2007).

While Part 2 examines the science underlying expressive movement, Part 3 explores the teacher's role in the development of young dancers' artistry, creativity and technical skills.

Part 3

# The art of training dancers

# 8  Our role as ballet teachers

When we think about our role as ballet teachers, we might ask ourselves what 'teaching ballet' actually means. Many answers may spring to mind, possibly referencing ballet's historical beginnings, its evolution through centuries and its current place as a well-loved performing art. Some teachers may cite technique and physical discipline as crucial elements. Others may focus on ballet as performance, as enjoyment or as an opportunity for self-expression. Even though ballet began as formal entertainment for the royal court, centuries of influences have enabled its development into a richly diverse art form. Given this diversity, teachers now hold diverging views of what 'teaching ballet' means in practice.

From a historical viewpoint, ballet's technique has responded to the dictums of influential ballet masters and teachers such as Pierre Beauchamp, who gave the world the five positions of the feet; Carlo Blasis, who codified the *grands poses*; then Enrico Cecchetti, mentor and teacher to Anna Pavlova, Vaslav Nijinsky, Tamara Karsavina, George Balanchine and many other iconic figures. Agrippa Vaganova formalised the Vaganova Syllabus, which underpins numerous teaching systems throughout the world, while Olga Preobrazhenskaya, herself an eminent ballerina, taught Irina Baronova, Tamara Toumanova, Alexandra Danilova, Maina Gielgud, Maurice Béjart and Margot Fonteyn, among others. These legendary teachers and their students seeded the perennial flowering of ballet and ballet teaching across the world. Each of them redefined their predecessors' approaches and changed expectations and possibilities regarding ballet technique. In this century alone, dancers have learned to safely perform technical feats that were previously regarded as impossible or, at best, unnatural and dangerous. Many leading teachers now embrace fitness training, which prepares and protects dancers' bodies as they exploit their full physical potential so they can meet rapidly expanding choreographic expectations. Some teachers are increasing their own knowledge so they can develop their students' psychological skills and consequently their ability to flourish in ballet's challenging environment. Today's teachers are now at the forefront of this lineage but, to participate in ballet's progress, we must also look to the development of ballet's artistic and expressive aspects.

Choreographers exert a profound influence on ballet by reflecting their social, cultural and intellectual environments as much as their personal creativity. Filippo Taglioni epitomised the Romantic Era with *La Sylphide* in 1832. Decades later, Marius Petipa encapsulated the grandeur of Imperial Russia in the first and third acts of his 1895 version of *Swan Lake*, while Lev Ivanov's choreography for the ballet's second and fourth acts signalled a new, more naturalistic and expressive approach. Ivanov's innovative choreography is likely to have inspired younger choreographers, including Michel Fokine, whose *Les Sylphides* leaves the formalism of Imperial Russia far behind. In the decades since, choreographers

DOI: 10.4324/9781003395188-12

have expressed, and sometimes rebelled against, socially relevant themes and aesthetics. Ballet choreographers now explore the physicality and expressivity of other contemporary dance styles, loosening and expanding the rules for what makes a good ballet dancer.

The new sounds, rhythms and structures of contemporary music have helped ballet break new ground, presenting opportunities far beyond those of conventional 'ballet music', so ballet choreographers now revel in exploring complex themes rather than simply telling stories. Today's choreographers and composers collaborate with designers to create new aesthetics – new visions of beauty and new meanings. Evolving aesthetic preferences influence ballet as much as they do fashion and architecture – the tiny dynamo dancers of the 1950s were superseded by the streamlined sylphs of later decades, and this new century has awakened to the glorious beauty of ballet dancers from diverse ethnic backgrounds. Given the breadth and depth of today's ballet world, there is no longer a simple hierarchy of excellence – each dancer, choreographer and teacher can only be measured by their aesthetics and their own goals. As a result, ballet now has a greater vibrancy and relevance than ever before.

Ballet teachers, too, must embrace this diversity. Ballet technique has left behind the past's simple criteria for excellence to embrace the many ways the moving body can create beauty, ideas and emotion. One might argue that a good *battement tendu* will always be a good *battement tendu* but, in fact, every *tendu* is slightly different from any other, as Bernstein's 'repetition without repetition' rule explains. The *battement tendu's* movement quality can change, the response to the music can change, the dynamics can change, the sensory impact can change, the coordination with breath may change. The relationship between the extending and the closing actions can vary. These differences give a simple *battement tendu* expressive and musical potential; they breathe life into a daily exercise and transform it into an artistic element, a choreographic tool, possibly an inspiration. One must only look at the 'Entrance of the Shades' in *La Bayadère*. As Marius Petipa intended, we see a mirage of identical spirits moving as one, hallucinatory visions of the dead Nikiya. If we look with a pedantic eye at the most 'perfect' performance, each dancer's arabesque is very slightly different from their previous one and very slightly different from each of the other dancers' arabesques. Yet, harmony of intention and musicality between the dancers can make this vision heart-achingly beautiful. We believe each of them is Nikiya. Our Mirror Neuron System allows us to participate in the dancers' unified intention as well as the sensory experience of their movement.

Given today's choreographic creativity and innovation, 'good technique' is a constantly moving target. Technical excellence is no longer a simple vertical measure. A dancer's technique must now be an emotionally, creatively and dramatically expressive tool, capable of transforming itself according to style, music and meaning, and serving as a source of inspiration for present choreographers and those yet to come. It is unlikely that any one teacher can provide a young dancer with every technical and artistic resource required for a successful ballet career, so ballet teachers can benefit by considering their own place within this expanding world and how they may wish to contribute to their students and to the art form. Equally important, a teacher can benefit by considering how they themselves may be enriched and challenged throughout their teaching career.

As teachers, we usually have a subconscious awareness of what drives us to teach, but it is well worthwhile taking time to identify our own overarching philosophy, our set of fundamental beliefs about teaching. It can be difficult to encapsulate personal beliefs in writing, but the resulting statement (possibly one sentence, a paragraph or a page) can provide a context for our general approach, day-to-day decisions and fundamental planning.

A statement of philosophy can guide the way we present our school and our classes to students, parents and the public, and it can serve as a 'tap on the shoulder' to question the wisdom of a potential action, statement or change of direction. Most importantly, it can influence the way we teach, the words we use, our definition of success and our relationship with students as they face the challenges and joys of learning ballet.

In many cases, high-achieving ballet students who do not progress to performing careers become ballet teachers, while some enjoy professional careers before becoming teachers. For many, the first step is to join a teaching organisation with a set teaching methodology or to join the staff of a ballet school with its own teaching system. Others may undertake training courses in ballet teaching. As a rule, these paths offer a structured system and opportunities for ongoing skill development and education. This sounds like a good arrangement – people who want to teach ballet learn what to teach and how to teach it – but it does not address the fact that each teacher is unique, with individual gifts, preferences and attitudes. Each student is similarly unique, and ballet itself has many faces – stylistic, expressive and technical. If we think back to a teacher who made a strong impact on us, even if we attended only one class with them, the defining factor is usually that they knew exactly who they were, what they could offer and how they wanted to teach – each had a strong personal philosophy. David Howard, Anne Woolliams, Marika Besobrasova and Johnny Eliasen can be counted among such teachers, and their lasting influence on countless students, dancers and teachers is profound.

While ballet teachers aim to teach each student as well as possible, a personal philosophy goes further than that. It is about clarifying what is special about your view of ballet, where your perspective is unusual, or possibly unique. We all carry in our hearts a teacher who 'raised the curtain' for us and revealed deeper truths than pointing our feet. As teachers ourselves, we can find our unique voices by searching for our personal philosophy regarding ballet, and teaching, and then re-evaluating it every few years. The world around us changes, personal events enrich or challenge us, and we become different people within a decade or so. Our view of ballet expands and deepens as new experiences and conversations enhance our insight. Refreshing our philosophy gives our teaching a new perspective and a new lease on life. Although philosophical statements can include the influences that led to our beliefs and our values in general, their main content is drawn from our responses to much simpler questions.

It may be wise to start the process by asking ourselves why we teach ballet. The complexity of this apparently simple question can be daunting. While no response is 'wrong' or unacceptable, it is worth exploring the possible effects of our motivation on the way we teach and consequently on our students. For many, the answer is obviously 'because I love ballet'. Indeed, many of us have a lifelong desire to be involved in ballet. At the same time, we should explore which aspect of ballet we love. Do we love an image of ballet we hold in our heads, possibly of beauty, of movement to music, of emotion, of magic, of athleticism or possibly of an ever-elusive perfection? Do we love the intricacies of ballet technique? Do we enjoy the physical sensation of dancing? Do we love mastering physical challenges? Do we believe learning ballet can be a fulfilling experience and, if so, how? Do we remember with fondness the relationship we had with our own teacher? Do we think the discipline of ballet can help children acquire discipline in other aspects of their lives? Do we long to train potential professional dancers? Do we believe every child should have the opportunity to experience the joy of dance?

The initial question may prompt some teachers to say, 'I want my students to love ballet as much as I did as a student'. Clearly, this is an admirable goal – it assumes you want to pass on to students the precious gift you received with your own training. Your love of ballet might lead you to focus on the most enjoyable aspects of class and to be creative in the ways you present exercises. However, students can be attracted by different aspects of ballet, and many students will never love ballet in the same way you did. For some teachers, this can be frustrating. One dancer remembered his early fascination with ballet as an intricate puzzle, endlessly revealing new insights regarding music, technique and expression. His intellectual side 'loved ballet' at least as much as his emotional and sensory sides did – and his fascination with the complexity of ballet now serves him well as a professional dancer. Focusing on finding the way into individual students' hearts and minds can make ballet fulfilling for them, and it can broaden our own perspective.

Another teacher with a different focus may say, 'I want to give students a strong ballet technique'. A strong technique is necessary for potential dancers, although the definition of 'strong' may be variable. Well-controlled turnout, flexibility, line, musicality, power, endurance and exceptional coordination can all be considered components of a strong technique. Students in vocational training have usually been selected for their capacity to thrive physically under the conditions that produce a strong technique, but many students who dance beautifully may not have the physique or mindset to make this a healthy option.

Developing a strong technique requires years of consistent, regular training, pushing past perceived, or sometimes actual, barriers and devoting substantial amounts of time that might otherwise have led to more rounded social experiences, access to further educational opportunities and a broader view of the world. This trade-off is unfortunate, because we all benefit when our artists are culturally aware and intellectually curious. However, if we re-interpret the word 'strong' as 'harmonious', the issue changes to some extent. Aiming for harmonious technique enables beautiful, expressive movement and a broad movement vocabulary without the dangers of pushing the body beyond its limits or reducing students' awareness of and participation in the world around them. Aiming for a strong technique is admirable, but the questions are whether any student in the class could be placed at physical risk and whether the required training coincides with each student's capabilities and goals.

A third response could be, 'My priority is to ensure my students are physically and emotionally safe at ballet'. This is another praiseworthy goal. Physical safety requires constant scrutiny of the environment (including unsecured objects, floor construction and surface, ventilation, access to toilets and drinking water), as well as ensuring safe student movement around and outside the school premises. Monitoring of pick-ups and unexplained absences or lateness demands time and vigilance, but they are essential aspects of young students' physical safety. Physical safety also refers each student's capacity to cope with the physical demands of the classes. Managing physical safety alongside the student's expectations can be difficult. A student's body may not be ready to manage new expectations such as *pointe* work or *pas de deux*, despite excellent general achievement.

Emotional safety can be more complex. A remark that initially seems innocuous can trigger long-term emotional hurt in children with personal problems at home or at school, or in those facing issues such as neurodiversity, gender diversity or racial discrimination. Children, and especially adolescents, can be adversely affected by student interaction outside or inside the studio itself. Teachers can never predict all the factors that may reduce a young person's sense of safety, so compassionate vigilance is essential. Many teachers do not have support staff on hand, so it is wise to plan the practicalities of dealing with emotional crises as well as nose bleeds and toilet emergencies.

A teacher with a developmental mindset may say, 'I want to help my students develop resilience and a sense of autonomy'. Given the high investment most students place in their training and their relationship with their teacher, ballet classes present ideal opportunities for fostering healthy coping mechanisms. Autonomy, self-awareness, resilience, problem-solving, critical thinking and other psychological skills are beneficial in ballet training and in the profession but, possibly even more important, they are invaluable life skills. Teachers can help students develop these skills within ballet classes, especially with the help of websites such as those that teach 'Psychological Skills in Ballet Training'.

Finally, a teacher with a different focus may respond with, 'I want each student to feel successful'. This goal requires careful consideration. A student whose definition of success is entirely focused on dancing the principal role in *Don Quixote* with a major ballet company is not likely to experience success at any time within the first five years. In fact, it is statistically unlikely the student will ever experience success as measured by this specific goal. Similarly, a goal of 100 *fouettés* is unlikely to be achievable, and pursuing it would probably waste time more usefully directed to less-spectacular but more intrinsic goals. At the other end of the spectrum, a student whose aim is simply 'to learn ballet', 'to have fun' or to accompany a friend, could lack motivation to continue beyond the first month or year. It is the teachers' responsibility to help each student set achievable short-term and mid-term goals. Young students may not be capable of setting safe, useful and personally achievable goals for some years, so teachers need to help them re-visit their goals whenever appropriate.

Having a student progress to an elite training institution or a professional career usually rewards a teacher with feelings of happiness, satisfaction and pride. We share vicariously in the student's success, and we feel validated in our ability to guide other students to similar success in the future. Even so, these occasions depend on the progress of select students, and they are few and far between. For our own happiness, and for the benefit of every one of our students, we need to formulate more varied criteria for our own success. A student who is anxious about their technical ability may struggle to improve their flexibility, tensing their muscles to force their body into the desired positions. If the teacher encourages the student to release muscular tension and rely instead on imagery, sensory awareness and breathing, the result is likely to be far-reaching. The student's technique is likely to improve, their problem-solving skills will develop and their confidence will increase. The student will be happier, and the teacher should rightly experience the warm glow of success. Strategies like this are lifeblood for teachers. We give our energy, our knowledge, our imagination and our passion to our students daily. Some students easily return this gift, delighting us with the way they flourish under our guidance. Other students may find ballet more challenging, but every student has the capacity to feel and communicate joy in their achievements. Identifying the key to each student's ongoing progress and sharing in their happiness when they overcome drawbacks can be profoundly rewarding for us as teachers, and well worth our effort.

These scenarios are likely to have stimulated still more questions and even more ideas about our own relationship with ballet, with teaching and with our students. Distilling these thoughts into a simple statement may seem challenging but, as teachers, we distil our ideas and the information we convey daily. We focus on selecting key points that will unlock learning rather than burdening our students with all the knowledge we ourselves have accumulated through the years. We also encourage our students to prioritise essential points before focusing on secondary issues. So, although the task of defining our own philosophy of teaching requires thought, it can provide reassurance and guidance in the years ahead. A philosophical statement is personal, for our own use alone. It does not need to follow any particular format, and it does not require any external approval. However, for those who would appreciate further guidance, the following fictional statements may indicate different approaches to the task:

*'I believe that ballet classes can provide a fulfilling and enjoyable educational experience for all children. Ballet classes can help children develop physically, emotionally and mentally, while developing their resilience and creativity.'*

*'In my view, dance is a fundamental aspect of being human, and all children deserve an insight into dance as a physical, emotional and sensory experience.'*

*'It is my belief that ballet classes instil the self-discipline and perseverance that are often missing in general education. Ballet's technical challenges can help children develop the resilience and problem-solving skills necessary for success in all walks of life.'*

*'I believe that ballet is the most beautiful experience a child can have. I want my students to develop a sense of beauty and grace in their own movements, and to enjoy ballet as an expressive art. I want children to feel empowered by their ability to express themselves through dance.'*

These sample statements do not place restrictions on how we teach or which system we teach. Rather, each represents a framework – a statement of personal priorities to guide us in responding to the many choices we face each day. Formulating our own statement is an exercise in self-awareness, helping us to experience first-hand the personal growth we hope to foster in our students. When we are exhausted and the demands of our chosen profession threaten to overwhelm us, re-reading our statement can reassure us in following our career path and help us to find new inspiration.

# 9 Skills in cueing and feedback

This chapter outlines the links between cueing methods, feedback and motor control, which enable dancers and students to learn new movements and to gain a new perspective on known movements. In general, the theories can be applied to contemporary dance or ballet, even when the examples refer to ballet-specific skills.

Physical demonstration, either by the teacher or another dancer, is the most common way to provide details of positions and movements. The learner absorbs the visual information through their Mirror Neuron System, sharing vicariously in the motor control that enables the movement and fulfils the movement's intention. This is obviously a quick and efficient way to transmit technical information, but it can be problematic when students are asked to mimic their teacher's or another student's demonstration. Each person's movement is unique. Differences in body proportions, bone structure, musculature and coordination affect people's positions and movement. People's temperament leaves its imprint too. Then there are issues of gender and age – it is clearly inappropriate for a young student to absorb the imprint of a mature teacher's movement.

Sometimes, students absorb their teacher's physical anomalies, possibly shoulder stiffness or neck tension, with all oblivious to the problem until another teacher or an examiner observes the class. Students are rarely able to discriminate between their much-admired teacher's inadvertent technical inaccuracies and the information they intend to convey, so technical faults such as dropped elbows in 2nd position can become embedded in students' motor control. The solution lies in merging physical demonstration with verbal description and explanation, supported by sensory and imagery cues.

Our motor systems respond to the purpose of a movement rather than its mechanics, so it is beneficial to describe tasks in terms of the movement's goal or aim. Introducing a *plié* by describing the isolation of both legs in their hip sockets, maintenance of turnout by activating the rotators, core stability and so on, overloads the short-term memory and results in confusion. As soon as general postural alignment has been established, a *plié* simply requires both kneecaps to face sideways throughout the bending and stretching actions. Trying to build guardrails against problems that may not arise is confusing, it freezes degrees of freedom unnecessarily and it overloads short-term memory.

> Simplicity is key to effective teaching—and to effective learning.

Good motor control depends on efficient coordination between the muscles' agonist and antagonist roles. Since it is impossible to achieve this through conscious muscle activation, it is preferable to describe movements in the motor cortex's own language, namely, imagery. Sometimes this may seem counterintuitive, because the obvious way to stretch the leg is to pull up (contract) the muscles at the front of the thigh. While it is true that the quadriceps (the group of four muscles in the front of the thigh) contract to stretch the leg, the hamstrings at the back of the leg should resist the contraction to ensure efficient, safe movement. For a weight-bearing leg, imagery of energy streaming in a straight line from the relevant sit-bone (one of the bony bumps you sit on), through the back of your leg and your heel and the floor triggers the motor cortex to coordinate all necessary muscles as efficiently and effectively as possible. When the leg is not weightbearing, or is on *pointe*, the energy should continue through the arch, the first two toes and beyond. Since muscles cannot lengthen by themselves, imagery focusing on the lengthening action ensures the agonist and antagonist work together, thereby enhancing coordination. Unfortunately, although strategies like these can improve performance, students can become fixated on adjusting the external appearance of their movement.

Dancers often rely on mirrors for feedback because the reflected image of one's body can reveal problems in position and line. However, conscious adjustments to your position or movement in response to your reflection in the mirror are much less effective than the fine, near-instantaneous 'online' adjustments made by the motor system in response to internal sensory feedback. In fact, it is estimated that it would take around a quarter of a second to see a problem in the mirror and then correct the movement (Karin et al., 2016). Adjustments as slow as this may help improve still positions, but mid-movement adjustments would lead to poorly coordinated jerkiness. Other problems arise. To see the reflection in the mirror, the dancer's eyes, and possibly head, must be oriented toward the mirror, thereby disturbing the harmony of the body parts, weight distribution and balance. The dancer will then learn this inharmonious position or movement. Unfortunately, conscious manipulation of body parts in the hope of creating a better image in the mirror is unlikely to equal the finely coordinated movement created by the sensorimotor system.

Mirrors can also lead to distorted evaluations. Dancers can become focused on their physical appearance instead of the movements and shapes they are making. An overly positive opinion of their own appearance may distract a dancer from the issue at hand, that of improving performance, and may deter them from exploring new approaches. However, it is much more likely that a dancer will focus ruthlessly on perceived negatives, seeing a distorted and unacceptable image of themselves that could lead to harmful behaviours. It is certainly not easy to ensure that mirror use will lead to productive outcomes in terms of technique or psychological and physical health, so any benefits should be weighed against a possible decrease in sensorimotor feedback and potential problems with body image.

Video recordings, possibly taken and viewed on a mobile phone, are a well-established means of evaluating movement after the fact. Options to adjust playback speed, to pause on one frame, to enlarge an image, and to replay various sections can assist dancers and teachers in analysing problems and suggesting solutions. Video is superior to looking in the mirror because the dancer does not need to adapt to the camera's position. This has the benefit of allowing the dancer to coordinate their head and eyes with the movement as they usually would. However, video recordings prompt the dancer to adapt the visual appearance of their movement rather than create new implicit cues, so they are unlikely to improve whole body coordination. The next technological step involves motion capture technology. This system uses many cameras to track and analyse a dancer's movement by recording the paths of up to 150 small reflective markers attached to their body. The resulting 3D computer images can be used to research dancers' movement patterns but the technology is too cumbersome, time-consuming and expensive for dancers' personal use. Its other disadvantage is its focus on the external aspect of the dancer's body and consequent inability to enhance implicit learning, expressivity or coordination.

Over the centuries, tactile feedback (touch) has played a large part in training dancers, and in coaching professionals. These days, many societies have strict rules regarding adults touching children and young people, so some schools prefer that teachers not touch students at all. It is wise to ensure students and parents are aware of the school's policy on tactile feedback and the teacher's position within that policy. In schools that permit touch, teachers may choose to do so after asking the students and their parents for general permission. Even if permission is given, teachers must ensure that their touch is not intrusive or overly assertive and that it adheres to professional and legal guidelines. In addition to official rules, teachers should inform their class about their specific approach and, if applicable, ask the class for general permission to give tactile feedback, noting anyone who appears hesitant or refuses. Wise teachers wishing to give tactile feedback quietly ask, 'May I?' before touching the student.

There are two potential benefits from tactile feedback. Firstly, the sensation of the teacher's hand on the relevant part of the student's body can combine with other somatosensory input to influence the student's movement, possibly by drawing their attention to unnecessary muscle tension or inaccurate placement. Using an indirect but more productive approach, a student can form new kinaesthetic imagery for controlling hyper-extended knees (knees that bend backwards). The teacher can exert pressure on the student's heel while the student feels a line of energy pushing from their sit bone, though the back of their knee, to and beyond their heel. To be beneficial, the teacher's touch should be expected by and be acceptable to the student, be gentle but firm, be steady and last long enough for the student to absorb the somatic information. Somatic information will be absorbed more easily if it is accompanied by very little or no verbal instruction. Given the teacher's authority over the student, the teacher's voice and cognitive information will inevitably be given precedence over the subtlety of somatic processing.

The second aspect involves any actual adjustment or manipulation of the student's body by the teacher. After placing a student's body in the required position, teachers often ask, 'Can you feel that?'. Teachers can feel frustrated when students respond, 'No', even after multiple attempts. The students do so because they might be able to see what their body is doing but their sensorimotor system, which both activates and receives feedback from movement, has not been involved. Other students say, quite honestly, that they can feel their body has been moved. Even so, since their bodies have been moved passively, their motor system does not know how to recreate the desired position, and their sensory system does not know how to recognise the desired position if they recreate it by chance. Research by David Ostry and his colleagues (2010) shows that participants whose limbs were moved passively to a new position showed no evidence of the sensory change necessary for motor learning (Ostrey et al., 2010).

Sports science research has produced a vast amount of information on feedback, and particularly augmented feedback (AF), which adds to, or augments, feedback from the sensorimotor system. For dancers, AF is usually given by a teacher or ballet master.

Concurrent feedback (feedback while the person is moving) may be useful if it identifies important markers that should be achieved. For example, the word *scoop* might encourage the dynamics of the *plié* before a *cabriole*, especially if the feedback is expected and the teacher's tone of voice and body mimic the quality of the *plié*. On the other hand, concurrent feedback should be used sparingly. Firstly, it attempts to influence a motor plan when it is already under way, so it threatens the dancer's coordination. Secondly, it distracts the dancer from all-important intrinsic feedback. It has been shown that athletes who rely on explicit feedback, especially if it is delivered verbally, are more likely to 'choke' under pressure than those who rely on intrinsic feedback (Otte et al., 2020). Sports science has also investigated many more aspects of feedback, beginning with Knowledge of Performance and Knowledge of Results.

Knowledge of Performance (KP) results from verbal, tactile or similar information designed to increase the dancer's awareness of how they are performing a movement. A teacher could say that the hip is lifted in *retiré*, the pelvis tilted too early, the shape of the movement is unsatisfactory, certain muscles are too tense or coordination between body parts is problematic. A teacher could also offer similar instruction through positive KP, highlighting the role of better pelvic placement in hip isolation, and advising a focus on the music to help with coordination. While dancers may benefit by hearing teachers analyse their movement, negatively presented KP can cause serious harm. Despite the teacher's words, dancers frequently receive negative KP from the teacher's or another person's visible reaction, ranging from a pursing of the lips to a hands-up expression of horror. Positively phrased KP is beneficial physically, and it also helps dancers feel positive about themselves as learners – an invaluable aspect of technical and artistic development. All teachers need to watch for dancers and students who are at low ebb in dance terms or psychologically. There is always some small but praiseworthy attempt or intention in need of reinforcement, possibly, 'That was a much better approach! I noticed you picturing in your mind how the pirouette would go – that is real progress! It's fine that you lost confidence as you started, everyone does that at first. Now you are good at practising it in your mind, you are ready for the next step.' Asking the student what might help their body do what their mind can already do may uncover a problem such as muscle tension, fear of falling over and looking silly, faulty imagery, or even a sore ankle or slippery shoes. If the student feels understood, they may be prepared to try again. At the other end of the spectrum, a student who has just executed their first double pirouette deserves to feel the achievement has been recognised, and an enthusiastic response such as, 'What an improvement! You should feel really happy about that!' should bring that warm glow of success while also stimulating their hunger to go further.

Knowledge of Results (KR) research has been primarily in sport or in other quantifiable skills such as hitting a target. In many sports, KR is focused on a medal and a place on the podium. Dance competitions and examinations might offer students similar black-and-white KR, but short-term goals can interfere with the integrity of the student's training and the dancer's performance. In addition, overtly quantifiable KR does not reflect the reality of ballet as an expressive art. In its simplest form, KR is probably unnecessary in dance. Falling on the floor during a double tour is ample evidence of a poor result, and only few teachers rub salt into the wound by saying, 'You fell over' or, even worse, 'You fell over again'. 'You fell over because your weight was too far back' may or may not help the dancer to avoid that problem, but the comment is negatively phrased and does not identify motor control and imagery factors that may be relevant. Alternatively, identifying the core of the problem, then suggesting a change in spinal alignment or a stronger push off the back foot may help frame 'falling over' as part of the learning continuum rather than a sign of ineptitude – an approach more properly labelled *KP*. Since dancing is not quantifiable on a vertical scale, and perfection is an invalid measure, KR may not be relevant to dancers.

Detailed verbal instruction before students start an exercise, verbal feedback while they are dancing and more verbal feedback as soon as they finish is a common strategy in ballet classes all over the world. It has been shown that too much verbal feedback is a form of 'overcoaching' that restricts beneficial movement exploration (Davids et al., 2008). According to Otte and colleagues, the coach (teacher) should not be the main problem-solver during practice. Rather, they should act as a moderator, guiding the athlete's (dancer's) own problem-solving when necessary (Otte et al., 2020). Ideally, feedback should be positive. As in other forms of learning, positive feedback encourages motivation, while negative feedback is not only discouraging, but it also reinforces the unwanted action in the dancer's mind. It is preferable to strengthen focus on actions that are likely to lead to success and to give feedback on successful attempts only, allowing poor attempts and their contributing factors to fade from conscious memory and from motor learning. Many research studies agree that positive feedback, or feedback after successful trials, 'boosts intrinsic motivation, self-efficacy and confidence, which in turn enhance effort, attention, and goal setting' (Lewthwaite & Wulf, 2010). However, highly skilled athletes who have well-established efficacy, and who are focused on refining high-level skills, may benefit from negative feedback about a specific factor that is interfering with their expertise (Magill & Anderson, 2014). That said, Magill and Anderson do not specify how the negative feedback should be given. 'You used enough energy this time, but your second leg was a bit late' is likely to have a different effect from 'Oh no, not again!! You always have your weight back! I keep telling you to keep it forward, but you never listen!' One approaches a negative aspect of the performance in a positive way, while the second option combines negative KR with a negative communication style.

Interesting research has examined the most effective times to deliver KP and KR. Again, studies have involved simple tests such as throwing a soft ball as far as possible with the non-dominant arm, so the results are informative but not necessarily transferable to dance. There are two types of delayed feedback (Magill & Anderson, 2014). The KR-delay interval is the interval of time between the completion of a movement and the presentation of KR. In a timing test, waiting for eight seconds before giving KR was much more effective than giving the result immediately (Liu & Wrisberg, 1997). These researchers proposed that instantaneous KR diverts the performer's attention away from the motor system's intrinsic feedback system. The post-KR interval is the interval of time between the presentation of KR and the beginning of the next trial. Eager teachers may see the KR-interval as the ideal time to deliver additional information, but dancers need time to process internal KR before they approach the next exercise. The teacher's silence can be golden.

As a note of warning to teachers and coaches, we should be careful in providing quantitative or qualitative feedback that may be erroneous. We may misinterpret the original cause of the problem – the neural, motor or physical 'fly in the ointment' that led to underperformance. Our concept of ideal performance may be coloured by our own image of performing the skill well, but each dancer is individual. Each dancer must develop their idiosyncratic way of performing a skill so that it eventually meets the standard for performance excellence. We must remember that dance is rarely quantifiable. A *développé* at 148° is not necessarily 'better', as in more beautiful or more expressive, than a *développé* at 140°.

Teaching is a balancing act between three variables: a) a student's understanding of and ability to perform a skill, b) the student's need for further assistance and c) the teacher's contribution towards the student's progress. The teacher's contribution may be high during the early learning period, but it should gradually decrease as the student's autonomy increases. Allowing a class to proceed from beginning to end without any feedback can be highly instructive for students and teacher alike. Students usually thrive when they can apply their own learning without interruption, and teachers can assess what has been learned and what still needs explanation. Rushing to 'fix it' is usually counterproductive.

As movement research progresses, it becomes evident that some of ballet's traditional protocols already incorporate scientific concepts. The effects of immediate feedback were compared with feedback after an eight-second delay (Karimi et al., 2019). They showed that immediate feedback resulted in better performance in early learning, but the eight-second delay resulted in much better retention of learning and generalisation of the learning to other similar situations. Other researchers also found that a few-seconds delay before feedback improved retention (Swinnen et al., 1990). They suggested that instantaneous KR might degrade natural error detection capabilities by blocking the dancer's spontaneous evaluation of the movement. In most ballet training systems, every formal exercise finishes with a simple movement coordinating the arms, head and breath – a reassuring return to 'home'. Depending on the speed of the exercise, this finishing movement may take between four and eight seconds. During the almost-meditative calm resulting from the finishing movement's simplicity and the accompanying music, the sensorimotor system has time to evaluate and improve the motor programs before the teacher's voice or the student's conscious thought start to interfere in implicit control. This quiet period is an invaluable part of skill learning. Waiting can be difficult for a teacher who is eager to help their students, but waiting will reap its reward.

Reduced frequency of feedback has been shown to benefit skilled performers. Time to think independently and to focus on intrinsic feedback and one's own problem-solving skills is essential to progress. Reducing feedback should encourage the development of autonomy, an important ingredient in performance excellence. It is advisable to inform students in advance of the reason for the reduced feedback. This is particularly pertinent in ballet, where some students depend on feedback from their teachers as validation of their personal worth as much as their performance.

Children use feedback differently from adults and, although adults benefit in accuracy and consistency when feedback is reduced throughout the learning period, children need longer practice periods and a much slower reduction in feedback. Researchers note that 'children who received 100% feedback during the acquisition phase were more accurate and consistent on a delayed retention test than children who received a reduced feedback schedule' (Sullivan et al., 2008). However, in a follow-up study, they found that children whose feedback had been reduced achieved the same standard as the 100% feedback group as soon as feedback was re-introduced. Unfortunately, the motor task in this study involved pulling a lever, and feedback was delivered by a computerized signal. It is possible that children would react differently with a more engaging task and feedback from a friendly human. Another highly relevant study showed that children begin relying highly on sensory feedback between seven and eleven years of age (Ferrel-Chapus et al., 2002). Since their study involved children drawing a shape in different orientations, it is relevant to dance only in supporting the wisdom of teachers balancing the degree of explicit feedback (usually verbal) against the developing child's growing ability to use sensory feedback.

> The goal of ballet training is for the dancer's movement to feel and appear natural, and this is achieved when the sensorimotor system manages the minutiae of movement control. Therefore, it is wise for teachers to gradually reduce verbal feedback during practice while encouraging students to be aware of and to trust their internal sensory feedback as it develops.

The complex coordination of multiple systems to produce efficient voluntary movement is astonishing but, for dancers, advanced movement skills are far from enough. As can be seen in the words that drive this book, dancers have a passionate desire to make their movement speak, to communicate with audiences.

# 10  Discovering technique

Throughout this book, technique has played a relatively minor part, and the dancers' quotes seem to place it as a contributing factor to their performance rather than an essential. However, technique is obviously important to dancers, especially ballet dancers, and the way they learn technique can have a profound effect on their dancing, and hence their careers.

At times in this book, the words *teaching* and *training* may seem almost interchangeable, but the differences are essential aspects of our work as teachers. In reference books, definitions of 'teaching' abound. Most are based on delivering information and strategies, although a few do focus on students' personal development. 'Training' usually refers to the development of skills and, in the ballet context, the development of ballet technique. In line with my personal philosophy, the following definition of teaching focuses primarily on the relationship between teacher and student, with the relationship between student and content (dancing) as the outcome. I see my role as providing the students with opportunities for 'discovery learning' – an approach developed by the educational psychologist Jerome Bruner whose beliefs can be paraphrased as 'Teaching is helping someone discover something'.

Within the ballet context, the teacher provides opportunities that prompt the student to discover ballet as a specific movement language. The focus is on guiding the student's growing understanding and development of motor control, creativity, musicality and artistry, rather than simply improving their physical capacity to perform exercises or dances. This learning will become increasingly relevant as the student progresses to professional challenges, both technical and artistic. While a focus on understanding and development will lead to increased technical skills, the reverse is rarely true. Naturally, these remarks are based on the author's personal philosophy, and other teachers may agree or may have a completely different approach. Either way, teachers' opinions will be in line with their own personal philosophies.

Again, according to this book's philosophical viewpoint and in contrast to 'teaching', 'training' entails helping the student discover how to achieve a high level of technical expertise. Ballet training should also aim to develop the student's stylistic and artistic ability. The training might be more or less rigorous, depending on the student's potential and goals. However, ballet training should always be supported by the skills and knowledge the teacher develops in ballet teaching, namely an understanding and development of movement, creativity, musicality and artistry. According to this philosophy, those who train students and potential dancers in ballet technique should see themselves first and foremost as ballet teachers, responsible for awakening students to the essence of the dance experience.

DOI: 10.4324/9781003395188-14

In turn, the students' discoveries will serve as a foundation for the specific requirements of advanced technical training and the profession.

*Art is about discovering what you believe is beautiful and sharing that with others.*

Artistry and creative skills begin with an understanding of the diverse ways the body can move, and movement's ability to express thoughts, emotion and music. Ideally, children explore their own movement potential before they start learning ballet, revelling in the exciting sensations of swinging, jumping, falling, floating, balancing, swaying, climbing, crawling, rolling and dancing, preferably free from adult observation or guidance. They discover the euphoria of leaning back as they swing; the fluctuating sensations of fall and recovery as they balance; the masterful power of their muscles; the tactile experiences of crawling under, over, around or through obstacles; the giddy thrill of spinning and the serene pleasure of floating. By discovering the integration of movement, sensory and emotional experiences, they develop the foundations for dance as an expressive art form. They are ready to discover ballet exercises as another expressive, exciting form of movement exploration.

*Right from an early age I had an instinct to arrange my movements in a certain way that would feel as pleasurable as possible. So when I was on stage, all I had to do was remember how I wanted to feel in a particular movement or step, and that would guide me.*

Whether children starting ballet classes approach their learning as a discovery experience or as a set of rules and physical challenges depends on their teacher. The mindset established in the first few years can easily become ingrained, colouring students' view of ballet and of their bodies, even when they move into the profession. Are our students' bodies and minds embarking together on discovering a new sensory and expressive language, and a broader aesthetic framework? Or are their minds aiming to impose external rules on their bodies' positions and movements?

*I did experience a time where I was in my head too much. Over-thinking and analysing every movement. It was a difficult and unsatisfying experience to overcome, but I did eventually.*

Ballet teachers need to embody their beliefs. Fortunately, this does not necessarily mean demonstrating an exercise or step exactly as the student should perform it. Students are perfectly capable of translating the qualities demonstrated by an arm gesture into a leg movement, especially if the arm demonstration is accompanied by the relevant breathing, expressivity, musicality, movement and voice quality. On the other hand, accompanying a movement demonstration with incompatibly forceful gestures and words, possibly thumping the body to highlight muscular effort, is a highly inappropriate method that stands in the way of harmonious, expressive technique. At best, a teacher's demonstration inspires the student to discover the most desirable movement patterns and expressive qualities in their own performance. A good teacher embodies the pleasure of exploration and discovery.

*A feeling of joy and freedom in movement*
*Spontaneity*
*Ease*

> A connection to the floor. Feeling grounded yet light
> Present in every moment
> Confident.

Coordination is the hallmark of excellent motor control in all vertebrates, and especially in dancers. Coordination has been defined as the distribution of muscle activation or force among individual muscles to produce a given motor task (Zatsiorsky & Prilutsky, 2012). Successful ballet dancers, like athletes, exemplify efficient coordination throughout their bodies, enabling them to perform an exceptionally wide range of movements without risk. Efficient coordination is the basis of dance, allowing the whole body to participate in expressing meaning, music and emotion, regardless of whether it is moving or still. Paradoxically, movement isolation is another core concept of ballet technique, even though isolation is not one of the motor system's preferred strategies in normal life. Although the motor system automatically shares movement between nearby joints, most ballet exercises require movement to be restricted to specific joints, leaving other joints and body parts blissfully unaffected by the movement. Understanding the difference between coordination and isolation is essential for teachers and for students.

In their first ballet classes, children's motor systems automatically provide safe, efficient, effective solutions to movement tasks. A beginner attempting to slide one foot to the side is likely to tilt their pelvis toward their supporting side, thereby sharing the leg movement between both hip joints and minimising wear-and-tear in either joint. It is important for teachers to recognise this strategy as proof of the child's healthy motor system rather than poor coordination, even though it disobeys the rules of ballet technique. Attempting to over-ride a natural response with muscular effort simply adds an additional action to oppose the natural action already under way. Cognitive instruction to 'keep your working hip down' does not cancel the original 'hip-up' motor plan, which will continue to interfere with the 'hip-down' instruction. These strategies create unnecessary stress on the body and produce effortful, uncoordinated movement. Even if the student appears to manage the exercise in the early stages, the muscle tension caused by conflicting actions is likely to interfere with turnout and extensions as training progresses.

Since the motor system's automatic solutions to movement tasks are deeply embedded, the best solution is to provide specific imagery designed to activate an entirely new motor plan. For young children, playing with jointed figures may help them visualise their body parts and alignment. Alternatively, a cardboard shape of a pelvis with legs attached at the hip sockets by paper fasteners can be useful in introducing the concept of weight placement. Henry Hips (or Peter Pelvis) might say he feels comfortable sitting on both legs but, when Lefty Leg goes out to play, Henry Hips feels better if he sits on top of Righty Leg. Showing Henry Hips' horizontal alignment while shifting his placement from two legs to one gives students a subconscious image of pelvic alignment. Strategies such as these seem simplistic, but imagery is one of the languages we use to communicate with our motor system and to over-ride automatic responses. To assist with this approach, creative skills prepare students' imagery and sensory awareness, enabling them to solve such conceptual problems as they arise.

Another vital aspect of coordination involves the degrees of freedom within the body's joints and their role in movement isolation within one joint or within a group of joints. Freezing, or co-contraction of the opposing muscles controlling a certain movement in a joint, can prevent movement in one or more directions. For instance, freezing the wrist's ability to perform up/down movements will still allow the wrist to move from side to side, while freezing both the wrist's degrees of freedom will prevent it from moving at all. Our capacity to carry out complex movements involving multiple body parts is due in part to our motor system's automatic control of many hundreds of degrees of freedom across approximately three hundred joints throughout our body. As an example, maintaining pelvic alignment while shifting the weight and isolating the working leg in *battement tendu à la seconde* is a major challenge for a relative beginner, and most students respond by freezing various degrees of movement around the hip joint. Research has shown that beginners automatically freeze more degrees in a joint than are necessary, and they are also likely to freeze movement in a few more adjacent joints, impeding compensatory actions throughout the body.

Another key factor is that the living body is never completely still. Ongoing functions such as breathing, blood flow, heart action, digestion and reflex actions influence the body's unstable structure, so any planned movement must occur within the context of instability. The complexity of this process cannot be over-estimated, but it is only one of the strategies the motor system uses to manage the body in the simplest and the most challenging movements, and all these strategies are far superior to conscious muscle activation. Even in the most basic technical exercises, conscious muscle activation is not capable of the complex coordination required for harmonious movement. Students who learn to rely on conscious muscle activation establish movement habits contrary to those created through natural processes. The motor system responds more efficiently to sensory and emotional cues than it does to information delivered through verbal instruction or by a teacher manipulating the student's body. Fortunately, the motor system responds readily to imagery, which is the perfect tool for erasing any conflict between natural processes and technical requirements.

Metaphorical imagery of a desired movement prompts the sensorimotor system to coordinate muscle actions in the most efficient, harmonious way possible. Various types of sensory imagery can help refine both technique and expression. 'Feel sunshine on your face' can encourage easy head alignment and a sensation of openness and confidence. 'Listen to someone whispering behind you' can improve spinal and head alignment as well as spatial awareness. However, the most useful may be kinaesthetic imagery – imagery of the sensory feeling of a movement.

> *I like to think about one particular feeling or shape whilst executing a step. It helps me to approach the movement in a way that works for me better than thinking about multiple technicalities at once.*

Imagery can solve most problems related to teaching and learning ballet. The only limitation may lie in the teacher's imagination, although the students' own imaginations can enrich the toolbox still further. Teachers who usually rely on factual descriptions may need to start by exploring their own sensory awareness – an important skill used by the sensorimotor system to plan and activate movement. Simply standing upright with eyes closed, then slowly moving the weight forward, back, sideways and diagonally, creates a multitude of sensations as pressure shifts around the feet and the muscles throughout the body respond to the changing demands. Moving the weight forward may feel as if a strong wind is pushing your body, or as if you want to see over a head-height wall, or as if your whole body is the minute hand of a clock, shifting from the hour to four minutes past the hour. In *chassé à la seconde*, you can feel as if your sit-bones are moving along a supermarket check-out conveyer belt. Your sensorimotor uses these images to ensure you achieve your goal. With practice, these 'as if' sensations can become an invaluable aspect of communication between teacher and student.

In general, moving (kinaesthetic) imagery is better than static imagery, and verbs support the sensation of movement. Feeling as if there is a straight steel rod from the top of your head, through your spine, and through the floor between your feet is a common but unappealing image, and it also negates the essential variability of motor control. Since the upright body is always in a state of movement, imagery should encourage a sense of fluid energy rather than a fixed action or position. Imagining a stream of energy flowing upwards from the floor, through the waist, between the ears and up through the sky activates the deep postural muscles. These small but highly efficient muscles, which provide the fluid stability essential for sitting, crawling, standing, walking and dancing, are readily activated by imagery. Students are likely to respond to movement-based images they are familiar with, possibly a waterspout or a firework piercing the night sky. Kinaesthetic imagery can help students achieve technical skills at a standard that is rarely obtained through other approaches, and this is particularly true in the case of turnout.

The traditional approach to increasing turnout is for the student to try to move their leg(s) from their previously achieved alignment to a more rotated position. Let us use *plié* as an example. Students pre-activate their established *plié* motor plan well before they begin the actual *plié* movement. As the *plié* begins, a student who is concerned about his turnout supplements his in-progress motor plan by consciously activating the muscles recommended to increase turnout. Conflict between the pre-activated and supplementary motor plans leads to unnecessary and ineffective muscle tension while also interfering with alignment and adding tension elsewhere in the body. Ideally, students who want to improve the way they perform *pliés* establish completely new imagery well before performing the exercise, and that image will be coloured by the music and the movements surrounding it. Let us consider turnout-enhancing imagery for *demi plié* in 1st position. A student may imagine the sit-bones at the base of the pelvis moving down and up again, as if it is being lowered and raised on an elevator or a forklift truck, thereby avoiding displacement of the pelvis. To improve turnout, it may help to imagine an elf pulling each knee sideways, then gradually releasing their pulling action as the pelvis rises and the backs of the legs lengthen. A similar approach is to imagine an eye on each kneecap, each looking to its own side throughout the bend and especially throughout the stretching movement. To improve a *plié's* depth as well as alignment, imagine a point two-thirds of the way up each shin. Let each of those two points follow a large arc towards a point on the floor far beyond the toes. When the shin points are not capable of following the arc any further, let them follow it back up again. All these images can be accentuated or softened by the coordination between the movement and the accompanying music.

Imagery can help movement, and technique, by encouraging more efficient and effective instructions from the sensorimotor system to the muscles. However, previous habits gained by chance or by prior training may interfere with the new instructions, sometimes leading to muscle tension and underperformance. In other instances, the student's body may not be capable of achieving the desired result, possibly due to bone or soft tissue limitations. If muscles are too short or tense to allow the required movement, well-designed imagery can encourage some degree of lengthening over time, especially if it releases counterproductive tension. Imagery cannot change bone structure that prevents the desired movement. For example, imagery cannot alter the shape of the bones in the hip joint, and any attempt to force change may lead to lifelong damage. The solution is to enhance all movement skills within each individual body's range, rather than setting up a perpetual 'war zone' between the motor system and the body's structure. Many famous dancers with limited *turnout*, from Anna Pavlova onwards, have achieved exceptional ballet careers through their movement quality, their expressivity, their musicality and their extraordinary artistry. With all this splendour in front of our eyes, degrees of turnout mean nothing.

Of course, ballet exercises are not simply mechanical. They are the vocabulary of our expressive language. Dynamics are an essential aspect – is a *plié* bouncy, smooth, energetic or powerful? Does it feel like a bouncing ball or a roller coaster, like jumping on a trampoline or swinging on a swing? As *plié* is an important part of ballet's vocabulary, emotion and expression also matter. Does this particular *plié* feel nervous, sleepy, brave, calm or dreamy? And finally, is the *plié* merging with the sensory and emotional feeling of the music? Is the student discovering the eloquence lying within each *plié*?

Possibly the most rewarding aspect of imagery is its ability to create solutions to movement problems from a child's first class, and throughout a professional dancer's career. Today's innovative choreographers envisage movement that lies well outside the parameters of technical training. Looking at Wayne McGregor's and William Forsythe's choreography, how do the dancers continually make exquisite lines that conform to ballet's aesthetic even though they may be extended in various ways, upside down, spiralling around each other's bodies, thrown through the air or sliding along the ground? The dancers are certainly not restricted by traditional ballet positions or movements, but they imagine the choreographic design through a classical aesthetic. The excitingly innovative result stretches our own imaginations – we see movement that is at once classical in its purity and groundbreakingly contemporary. It arouses emotion and ideas not usually inspired by ballet's conventional movements. This transformation of classical movement is liberating for choreographers, for dancers and for audiences. We, as teachers, should help students embrace the classical aesthetic within technical exercises, but also guide them in exploring how the aesthetic might be extended and manipulated to express contemporary ideals. Ballet training should open students' minds and bodies to the diverse potential of their artistic futures.

Children are movement experts long before they start ballet classes. Their imaginations and their motor systems solve most challenges implicitly, without the involvement of conscious thinking, and we teachers should try to enhance rather than over-ride these natural processes. In normal life, a child approaches an unfamiliar action with a simple image of the movement's purpose and parameters. A child's purpose might be to cross a quick-flowing stream by leaping from one bank to the other. By the time they are ready to take on the task of crossing streams, we can hope the child's motor system has created general motor programs for stepping, for jumping and for climbing stairs. We can also hope that the child looks at the surroundings to evaluate the task's parameters – the stream's width, its depth and possible dangerousness, and probably the stability of the ground for take-off and for landing. The child is unlikely to process all this information consciously, but their motor system will be busy assessing conditions and transforming and amalgamating existing motor programs to achieve the desired outcome. If the task is not beyond the child's physical capacity, they should jump the stream and continue on their way, safe and dry. Implicit control has achieved exactly what the child wanted, seemingly by magic.

Now we can consider how we, as ballet teachers, might help the child cross the stream. We may urge them to bend their knees, to move their weight toward their toes, and to lean forward before jumping. We could encourage them to push off with their legs, contract their gluteal muscles and stretch their body slightly mid-jump then bend their knees again as they land. We might suggest they take their arms back before jumping, then use them to stabilise their body in the air and swing them forward on landing. Maybe we would recommend breathing in beforehand, then out during the jump, while keeping their eyes on their target landing place. If this child is a ballet student, we might suggest they 'engage their core' throughout. Strategies such as this, where the aim is to control the body through cognitive instruction, are called explicit teaching, while the child is being asked to engage in explicit learning.

Implicit learning is the way we acquire our earliest movement skills, and we continue to rely on implicit learning throughout life. We discover how to operate a new tin-opener or an unfamiliar phone, we find our way around road closures, we work out how to undo a knot in our shoelaces and we usually manage to spoon soup into our mouths. We have evolved to learn implicitly, employing imagery and trial-and-error to acquire new skills and knowledge. In evolutionary terms, explicit learning is a more recent addition to our mental skills, with few benefits and a considerable number of disadvantages when applied to learning ballet technique. Therefore, teachers may find it beneficial to consider which type of learning they should encourage for any specific goal.

While we can never know exactly how Pierre Beauchamps taught Louis XIV his much-admired new ballet steps, ballet master Carlo Blasis's (1830) book, *The Code of Terpsichore*, appears to promote explicit rules about the use of the body, delivered by explicit teaching methods. Since then, most major teaching systems have been based on explicit teaching methods, and explicit assessments of progress – what the student can do, whether the student's movements obey the set rules. However, some outstanding teachers, being inspired to use a more implicit approach, have moved against the tide and trained exceptionally fluid, expressive dancers. It is to be hoped that this book supports and encourages teachers who feel instinctively that an implicit approach engenders intuitive learning and inspires safer technique and greater artistry.

> *When performing happens without thought is when dancing truly feels like speaking.*

Like the first child jumping the stream, an implicitly focused student responds to a movement's purpose and parameters. Since implicit learning is our primary method of learning, one might expect that new students will approach ballet technique from an implicit viewpoint. Unfortunately, the whole mystique surrounding ballet as a highly elite art form with a punishingly difficult technique deters students from trusting their instinctive movement systems – sadly, they feel they must devalue and ignore their natural tendencies in order to be 'special enough' for ballet. Teachers become experts by knowing every technical detail, including the muscles that support each of the various technical requirements. While this explicit knowledge may be useful for a teacher, transferring it to students is rarely wise. The motor system has evolved into an exquisitely efficient, economical and effective movement process, and this system relies on implicit cueing. Cognitive or explicit cueing, as described in the mythical teacher's instructions to the second child jumping across a stream, relies on conscious muscle activation – a poor substitute for implicit learning.

> *These days there is so much emphasis on anatomy in regard to dance training and conditioning, which is wonderful for injury prevention, although now as a teacher I am aware not to use that language too much. It's relevant in certain situations, but I think it's challenging and confusing for the body to respond when thinking about individual muscles. Imagery, analogies, actions and use of energy is a more creative way to achieve a more synergistic movement quality, which is what dancers need.'*

An important aspect of the teaching-learning transaction is the relationship between teacher and students. Ballet classes are necessarily hierarchical to some degree – it is extremely unlikely that students would ever discover how to become technically proficient without a teacher's leadership and guidance. Even so, the teacher/student relationship can vary immensely. Traditionally, ballet teachers were to be admired, revered and even feared as gatekeepers to success in class and an eventual ballet career. Praise or negative criticism from these teachers could lighten a student's heart or punch holes in their self-esteem. While the extreme version of the all-powerful ballet teacher is less common now, many of today's students still feel totally dependent on and subservient to their teacher. The teacher knows everything, and the student's job is to learn that everything and to perform that everything exactly as the teacher wants. Considering the number of hours serious ballet students spend in the studio, and their utter determination to do whatever they think is necessary, one can see that this is not a healthy learning environment for adolescents.

*It was clear the teachers didn't think I was good enough, they preferred their best students and made it obvious that they thought no one else was deserving of their time and attention. I didn't realise that the way ballet was taught was eating away at me – I was happy to be dancing! This speaks to the phenomenon that dancers will put up with anything just so they can dance.*

Although the 'teacher-as-benevolent-dictator' may help students acquire correct technique and meet external measures of achievement, it will not help them to dance in its fullest sense, or to discover ballet as a powerful means of self-expression. For this, students need to feel their ideas, opinions and problem-solving ability are recognised and valued. This means students must have opportunities to discuss their discoveries and difficulties with other students and with the teacher. The process may take a little time in class, but it produces rewards far outstripping those gained by repeated focus on the rules for good technique. Teaching resources such as 'Psychological Skills in Ballet Training' can assist teachers in adding this important dimension to their ballet classes.

Thanks to their Mirror Neuron System, all dancers are familiar with intended or unintended feedback from external sources, with another person's facial expressions, gestures, touch and verbal comments being the most obvious. Generally, teachers convey much more than they realise. Even before a word is said, students read the unspoken language of a teacher's posture (arms crossed or open, leaning forward or back, turning away, tense or relaxed), along with their movement dynamics, physical distance from students, the presence or absence of eye contact and tone of voice. Students may also feel uncomfortable or unsafe when confronted with a teacher's non-Duchenne smile. All this conveys infinitely more to students than the teacher's words.

Even though verbal communication plays an important part in giving students facts or advice, the actual words we use have wide-ranging effects. A prime example is the use of the words *perfect*, *correct*, *good* and *right*, alongside the dreaded *wrong*, *not good enough*, *incorrect* and even *bad*. Many teachers give students 'corrections', and students have been known to call their ballet school the 'House of Corrections'. There are several problems with this approach. Given the endless variability in students' bodies and the non-repeatability of human actions, there can be no absolute 'correct', 'right' or 'perfect' model. Learning, particularly in areas involving motor control, is not a linear process. Unlike solving multiplication problems, progress in learning technique is not countable – it ebbs and flows as new learning temporarily challenges previous learning, and an apparent lack of progress is almost always a period of consolidation, as new learning is absorbed into the existing knowledge base. Most students are instinctively aware that learning is a matter of exploration, so being told what they are doing is wrong and needs correction is frustrating. The very word *correction*, with its hint of the penal system, names a student's performance as unacceptable. Students will be well-served if teachers refer to 'improvements'.

> Replacing the word *correction* with *improvement* is a much better approach from a psychological point of view, especially as it supports students' understanding of the learning process.

Very small children coming into their first ballet lesson, bright-eyed and proud of their new 'ballet clothes', can inspire a nurturing, caring response in ballet teachers – 'Just look at my adorable little students!'. The instinct to care for the young and vulnerable is praiseworthy as long as it does not trap the growing student in a dependent role. 'Show me how well you can balance', 'I want you to point your foot', 'Will you turn out your leg for me?', 'I would like to see a nicely stretched leg' and 'Do it for me' abound in ballet classes, and these phrases are even common in the profession. But what is this language saying to the student or dancer? Firstly, the language implies ownership, harking back to the impoverished orphans in France's first ballet school. The approach places students as the teacher's property, with a duty to please their owner. Secondly, it infantilises the student or dancer, as if they were incapable of forming and achieving goals for their own satisfaction. Certainly, teachers play a prominent role by providing feedback and advice on overcoming difficulties. Teachers facilitate learning, but the student alone owns the learning. Like parents, teachers should gain pleasure from watching their students step towards self-sufficiency.

It is easy for teachers to lose sight of additional challenges faced by students as ballet training progresses. In-depth learning, required from students from puberty onwards, demands a great deal of energy. Teachers are usually aware of the physical demands of different exercises, and they plan carefully to increase students' endurance and strength over time. However, teachers are often unaware of the energy required by the CNS to manage increasing motor demands while controlling a body that seems to change from day to day. At any one time, each student in the class will be facing different developmental challenges, including short-term decreases in strength and coordination. Music can be a lifeline as students navigate their adolescent changes. As a sensory experience, music assists sensorimotor learning, and students need mental space to process its dynamics, rhythm, phrasing and emotional impact. Adolescent students need regular periods of silence in class if they are to learn efficiently and perform at their best. Many teachers maintain a running verbal commentary while students perform exercises, possibly under the misunderstanding they are helping. The commentary almost always repeats information given before the exercise started. Other teachers are inclined to call out 'Better!' or 'Good!' at random. The only way the student can pay attention to this distraction is by interrupting their motor control processes, thereby reducing their learning. Some teachers count or clap or stamp loudly to emphasise the musical beat – a strategy that overrides the student's ability to listen to the music and to process the sensation of their movement. Wise teachers offer students periods of silence, so their sensorimotor systems have time to solve movement problems without verbal intervention.

Teachers have the best intentions when they intrude on their students' learning processes. They want to give everything they can to support their students, to remind them of anything they might possibly have forgotten since the teacher last spoke and to ensure their students' success. Although this behaviour may appear to be supportive and may satisfy the teacher's urge to help, the student can experience it as a subtle form of bullying. A better strategy is to allow students to process the exercise silently before performing it, then watch without commentary to see any adjustments they make during or afterwards. Finally, each student benefits enormously by several seconds of silence and stillness after the exercise finishes, where the motor system can evaluate the motor plans and the student can allow their learning to consolidate before thinking consciously about possible improvements or about the next exercise. This way, the teacher can see clearly how much the students have absorbed, and which concepts still need development. It is important to avoid trying to teach anything that the students have already learned. Rather, students should be increasing their ability to conserve information and to apply it as needed. Teaching should be a continual process of 'letting go', driven by a desire to see students take flight as self-sufficient dancers. This is key to students' self-sufficiency – a basic requirement for dancers and for success in any field.

# 11 The speaking body

Laurel Martyn, a ballerina, a choreographer and my teacher, always supported my instinctive belief in dance as an emotional language. Her classes, like her choreography, allowed each of us to find an individual meaning within the movement and the music. Her approach had a profound effect on my own dancing and teaching and, consequently, on my fascination with the body's natural expressivity. Children are experts in movement as an expressive language long before their first birthday. Even before they begin to smile, their movement attracts our attention and lets us know how they feel, while their bodies' skill in expressing joy, anger, hunger and love becomes more articulate as they develop. Children move for the sheer pleasure of moving, to express their emotion and as a response to music but, for some unknown reason, we usually wait until a child can add leg actions before we label this expressive movement 'dance'. Movement also plays a complementary role with verbal language – emphasising, nuancing or showing ambivalence according to the words' emotional content. The expressive nature of movement remains throughout life, bringing joy in private and social settings and enriching our verbal and non-verbal communication.

Figure 12.1 shows dance as the culmination of a symbiotic relationship between movement, emotion and music, supported and modulated by respiration. Even though Part 3 of this book focuses primarily on ballet teachers and teaching, we must never forget that ballet is, first and foremost, dancing. Questions arise:

- How has ballet become synonymous with technique?
- Why is music often relegated to the role of accompaniment?
- How has emotion become reserved for performance, rather than being integral to the act of dancing?
- Is it possible to use the expressive, creative and sensory aspects of children's spontaneous dancing as the foundation for ballet technique?

One of the dancers contributing to this book remarked, 'It is so difficult to separate emotion when music and dancing are involved', but unfortunately it is rare to find ballet training that recognises the essential interdependence of these three elements. It is the teacher's responsibility to integrate music, emotion and movement from the first class and throughout every class. This is not only a fundamental aspect of learning for those students who may become professional dancers or teachers, but it is also the right of all students to

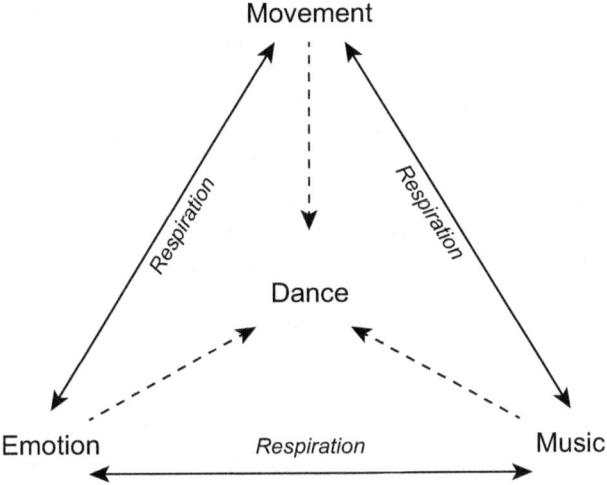

*Figure 11.1* Components of dance.
Source: After Bernardi et al., 2017.

experience the synthesis of music, emotion and movement that make dance such an important part of human expression.

> *If it were a particular emotion I had to express within the story and my character in a ballet, I would usually create that emotion in my body, and craft it to be either theatrical or raw and natural.*

Breathing, movement, music and emotion also assist in teaching harmonious, expressive technique. Here, we explore the place of breathing within the development of the technical aspects of dance. Firstly, it is important that students do not force their breathing in any way during exploratory exercises or while they are dancing. In normal life, our breathing adapts to movement challenges, music and emotion, even though we are rarely aware of it. If a person places a box in our hands, we may inhale with delight, exhale with sorrow, gasp with surprise or hold our breath with fear – all natural respiratory responses to various emotions. In dancing, the task is to become more aware of the different ways our breathing can respond to and coordinate with natural movement and with technique. The following approaches may help.

Students can quietly observe their breathing while standing still, then notice any changes as they slowly bend to touch the floor and return to standing. As they bend, they are likely to notice their diaphragm, ribcage and lungs becoming compressed to some extent, so they automatically breathe out. As they stand up, their lungs and diaphragm have room to expand and the air flows back in. After experiencing this natural coordination, students can explore the different effects of breathing, possibly by reversing their automatic pattern or by varying their breathing pattern during each movement. They can experiment with different breathing patterns in various technical exercises. Imagery can facilitate changes in breathing while avoiding force. As an example, it is natural to breathe in as you stretch your hand to reach a high shelf. Now, place your hand on a shelf at chest height, then bend your knees so your body sinks below your hand. You are likely to find that you exhaled in response to bending your knees, even though your hand rose above your body. Next, try breathing in as you rise to *demi-pointe* and breathe out as you lower. Then, breathe out as you rise and breathe in again as you lower. Did your breathing affect the feeling of the rises? Did you feel steadier on *demi-pointe* when you breathed in or out? In general, it may help to imagine your breath as a sequence of continuous curves of various lengths and depths. This sequence can be superimposed on the movement sequence in various ways, so a slow exhale may link a few movements, or one movement may link a few breaths. The brain automatically produces certain breathing patterns for standard actions, basing them on functional economy – maximising energy resources and minimising wear-and-tear on the physical body.

Since the general rule is to breathe out as you bend and in as you extend, the most obvious strategy for a *grand plié* is to breathe out on the way down and in on the way up. Unfortunately, this leaves little air in the lungs exactly when you need additional power to push the full weight of the body up to its original position. Ballet technique poses many similar challenges with no 'correct' response. In the case of a *grand plié*, the change from breathing out to breathing in could be initiated just before the full depth of the *plié* or at some other point. Breathing in a *cambré de côté* could ebb and flow throughout the bending and stretching actions, colouring the sensory effect felt by the dancer and the observer. *Développé* to *arabesque* can vary in technical efficiency, ease, and aesthetic and emotional impact according to its coordination with breathing. *Grand allegro* offers countless options, all resulting in different dynamics. Since many students hold their breath during difficult exercises, exploring different breathing patterns can lead to new vitality and ease. Sensory awareness of the relationship between breath and movement is key to developing movement dynamics, which in turn brings expressivity and musicality to the simplest and the most complex exercises and choreography.

Sadly, ballet training can reduce the innate relationship between music and movement to 'keeping in time' and 'dancing on the beat'. As breathing is integral to both movement and emotion, strengthening students' awareness of the links between these two and music promotes learning in all areas. Notwithstanding the expense, engaging a live pianist is probably the most effective way to enhance students' musicality while also adding artistic benefit and pleasure to each class. If this is not possible, the regular use of unfamiliar recorded music can widen students' experience of musicality in dance. By coordinating breathing with music in various ways, then adding simple movements, students can discover the resulting 'colours' and emotions. The integration of music, breath and movement is encapsulated beautifully by one of the contributing dancers, along with the sense of discovery lying at the core of artistry.

> *I even play with the counts a little, shape them and create moments either side of the notes in the music, where there is space in between to fill with microscopic movements. Or sometimes finding stillness within the notes, or in between steps, where there may be opportunity to find a moment in time or actual space to pay attention to a different part of the body, or to take a breath, or a different angle of the head.*

Emotion affects our breathing daily: a small gasp of surprise, an exhalation of relief, a sigh or even a groan of boredom. In dance, the word *emotion* is sometimes taken to mean major categories such as happiness, grief, ecstasy or terror, but the word also covers sensations more often referred to as 'feelings', such as 'I feel a bit gloomy today'. Although the link between breath and emotion may seem to be automatic and so irrelevant to a discussion about teaching, it is the foundation of expressive dancing. Therefore, breath and emotion should be considered essential components of technical training. This approach does not suggest forcing or standardising breathing patterns. Equally, it does not suggest overt shows of emotion or necessarily showing expression through the face, but simply the inner experience of emotion evoked by various movements, music and breath in different circumstances. Depending on breathing patterns and the accompanying music, an exercise may arouse a feeling of energy, brightness, dreaminess, light-heartedness or even melancholy. In turn, the experience of emotion influences our breathing and our movement. A *petit allegro* exercise can be transformed by a hint of silliness, happiness or mischief. Class, like a performance, can inspire a kaleidoscope of emotional colours, all supported by changes in breath.

I have already written about people's ability to detect fake smiling, and the detrimental psychological effects on people who are required to smile constantly. I have also mentioned two different approaches to emotion and expressivity that are common in ballet classes – that students should 'leave their emotions at the door' or that they should smile throughout all exercises. If students have been adversely affected by either of these approaches, focusing on breath, music, emotion and sensory awareness may help to override any previous harm.

As I stated previously, dancing and all other voluntary movements are regulated by the sensorimotor system, which integrates all the sensory, motor and other elements required for interaction with the environment. Although most students' sensory awareness regulates their normal range of movement efficiently, a much higher level of sensory awareness is needed for progress in the technical and artistic aspects of ballet. Some teachers and their young beginners may be eager to start with their first ballet class with 1st position of the feet, followed by *bras bas* and *plié*, because 'that's what ballet is!'. The potential downside is that the children learn what these positions and movements are, while being oblivious to how they feel. They may learn how to mimic a 'correct' position or movement, basing their assessment of 'correct' on their teacher's evaluation and (later) on their image in the mirror. In other words, they may not have acquired a sensory understanding of what they are doing and why a particular version is preferred. True learning occurs when children can discriminate between the sensory experiences embedded in one approach to a movement or position and compare these with the sensations evoked by other approaches.

There are many ways to encourage this sensory learning. Some teachers place a student's body into the required position or guide it through the required movement, then ask the student whether they can 'feel' the 'correct' position or movement. Students who have not developed sensory awareness are unlikely to feel, or be aware of, a relationship between body parts, an articulation of specific joints or a release of tension when the body is placed passively. The motor system does not recognise a position it has not created, so it cannot reproduce the position on demand. Therefore, the students are only likely to recognise feelings of discomfort or pain, which could be caused by muscle tension or conflicting motor actions. If a student replies that they can feel the position or movement, they could really be saying they can feel an ache or stiffness in their hip or a pain in their back. With no frame of reference, the student learns to welcome feelings of aches, stiffness and pain as proof of progress, thereby setting themselves up for long-term damage.

Training in sensory awareness and kinaesthetic imagery can be fun for young children. A jointed doll or artist's mannequin with flexible limbs can help them visualise and analyse their own movements. Arrange the sections of each leg in a random fashion – for example, one knee turned out with the foot rotated inwards, and the other leg in another misaligned position. Children usually recognise the incongruity of misaligned limbs. Ask whether the doll can stand up on two feet or on one foot with their legs like that and, if not, what might help the doll.

Next, let young students experiment with different ways of aligning each other's and their own legs and feet, taking care not to label well-aligned legs as 'perfect' or 'correct' and others as 'wrong' or 'bad', because the intention is for the students themselves to recognise the sensation of greater stability in a certain alignment then store that sensation in their sensorimotor system for further use. Ask students what happens if their knee faces in a different direction from their feet. Ask them to check whether changing their knees or feet makes their bodies and hips change too. They will soon understand that they are more stable if all segments are in a line. Ask them to stand with their feet parallel and slightly apart (for balance) then bend their knees, experimenting with various alignments until they discover stable leg and foot alignment. Let them label this 'magic legs' or any term you prefer, and encourage them to discuss what it feels like. In the next class, ask the children to stand with their legs slightly apart and their feet comfortably turned out. Let them discover which alignment feels like 'magic legs' did.

From there, the same process can be used in all basic positions and movements: Are their feet still placed well on the floor? Has their body changed? The same process applies to spine alignment. Anterior and posterior pelvic tilts are not abominations; they are simply options that are less successful in ballet than a neutral spine, as it requires less energy and makes the body feel lighter and looser. Children will revert to their formerly preferred alignment at times, but re-exploring the range of possibilities strengthens their knowledge. Every time they check and/or amend their alignment, they strengthen their kinaesthetic imagery and their sensory awareness – both of which are vital for dancers. As stated previously, learning ballet is a very slow process, but taking time yields better results.

Teachers may distrust this approach because their own bodies do not respond to the exercises as suggested. Our bodies are the sum of all the influences and demands they have incurred during our training and throughout our careers, whether they involve dancing or teaching. If we keep using an unsuccessful strategy for some time, the strategy becomes embedded in our motor system. When we try a new strategy, embedded motor actions linked to the unsuccessful strategy are likely to interfere. The old belief that more is better is likely to encourage us to try harder, thereby entrenching counterproductive muscle tension. Overcoming deep-seated problems like this takes understanding, time and patience, as we need to return to our 'beginner' self before we can build a new 'learner' self.

> A student who 'feels' and can change any misalignment early in their training will require much less monitoring by the teacher over the years ahead. The time taken establishing sensory awareness is in fact time saved.

To explore sensory awareness with breathing, ask students how they feel physically when they change their breathing (breathing normally, holding the breath in or out, or varying their breathing). Next, ask them how they feel when they change their breathing as they take the arms up to 5th position and return to *bras bas*. Steer the discussion beyond 'good' and 'bad', so they discover a wider range of sensations. These might possibly include 'energetic', 'weak', 'proud', 'brave', 'exhausted', 'sad', 'scared' or 'shy'. Later, ask them to notice their emotion when they coordinate their breath in various ways with movement of their own choice. This strategy can be used in any movement as their technique develops, thereby helping them discover the relationship between breath, movement and emotion.

> Sensory awareness of the interaction between music, breathing, movement and emotion is the foundation of artistry.

When focusing on sensory awareness, music and emotion, ask students to remember a short movement phrase, then ask them how they feel when they perform it accompanied by counting or clapping. Next, ask them how they feel when they perform the phrase with music. Compare that with how they feel when they dance the same phrase with different music. Ask whether the music changed their breathing, and whether music, emotion and breathing might be related. While these introductory exercises may seem unnecessarily time-consuming, they establish musical and sensory awareness that can be used and enhanced throughout their training. In all exercises and throughout class, it is helpful to establish the concept of dancing 'with' or even 'within' the music, rather than 'to' the music. Although the distinction may seem pedantic, dancing to music implies moving alongside the music, whereas dancing within the music gives the sense of merging the two.

> *Music is always an important influence for me; it is what facilitates my joy of dancing and creates emotion.*

Martha Graham, a supremely expressive modern dancer in the early 20th century, frequently said, 'Movement never lies'. Even so, the entire body can be as expressive in stillness as in movement, as countless sculptures, paintings and photographs prove. The body's posture, especially the angles, lines and curves created by various body parts, can reveal emotions and thoughts. Although the face can be expressive, emotion is more convincing when it is expressed through the body. It may be more relevant to this book to rephrase Martha Graham's statement as 'The body never lies'.

Some students prioritise technical proficiency throughout their training then layer their movement with facial expressions appropriate to the dance's meaning in rehearsals and performances. The resulting discrepancy between the messages from the body and the face can make audiences feel slightly uncomfortable, as if the dancer is being dishonest. How, then, can teachers train dancers so that their bodies speak the truth? The solution involves incorporating music, meaning, emotion and breath as fundamental aspects of technique. Ideally, the process should begin at a child's first lesson and develop consistently throughout training. If the teacher regards movement as an expressive language, this belief will permeate their words, gestures and demonstration, and students will hear, see and explore the expressivity of ballet technique in every class. Martha Graham wanted her dances to be 'felt' rather than 'understood', so they could reveal meaning and emotions not expressible through words. Her approach predicts motor control research, which differentiates between communication through the senses (feeling) and through cognition (understanding).

Expressivity in dance depends partly on the body's ability to express thoughts, emotion and music through movement, but it also depends on creative skills, defined here as an understanding of the infinite number of ways the body can move, even within the framework of ballet technique. Ideally, children explore a wide range of movement experiences from their earliest years, experimenting with climbing under, over and through obstacles and structures, swinging, leaping, running and hopping, skipping, rolling and tumbling, spinning, dancing and creating imaginative body shapes. If children discover how to perform these skills without coaching or 'help' from adults, their motor systems develop their capacity to achieve any desired movement in the simplest and most efficient way. Unfortunately for many children, contemporary lifestyles reduce the time and conditions available for exploring their physical potential, and so their natural movement skills are not always well-developed by the time they start ballet classes.

Teachers who recognise a lack of experience and skills in their students may be hesitant to add yet another factor to the content of their ballet classes, and they may hope ballet exercises will provide all that is needed. A creative approach to teaching can camouflage insecure skills in the early stages, but these skills will always hamper the development of well-coordinated and expressive dancing. On the other hand, any time devoted to children's creative skills is repaid by their increased ease in acquiring technique and their deeper pleasure in dancing. Creative skills training can help all children extend their natural movement skills as a basis for learning technique, while enhancing their ability to integrate movement, music and emotion. Creative skills training may begin with the student creating a body shape, or position, then becoming familiar with the shape through:

- Sensory awareness (what the shape or movement feels like);
- Sensory imagery (what their next shape or movement will feel like);
- Visual imagery (what a shape and or movement looks like or will look like);
- Problem solving (planning movement paths that will move the body from one shape to another).

As will be seen in the following examples, creative skills training is based on implicit learning. Creative skills training can be adapted according to students' ages and technical levels, and sessions can range from five to thirty minutes or more, depending on time availability. Regardless of the schedule, students will derive most benefit if teachers retain the words they use for concepts of sensory awareness and imagery, visual imagery and problem-solving while they are teaching technique. A teacher could preface a *plié* exercise by asking the class to suggest imagery. One may suggest a playground swing, especially the sensation of gathering momentum on the way down and releasing it on the recovery, or another student might suggest pushing a beach ball under the water then slowly allowing it to rise again.

*Battements tendus à la seconde* might be imagined as slicing cucumber, and this imagery could open discussion regarding the position of the imaginary blade in the moving leg. Sensory imagery of a blade running from sit bone, down the back of the leg, through the hamstrings, back of the knee and calf to the back of the heel supports stable leg alignment in parallel position. Rotating the image 90°, so the blade faces sideways, prompts the motor system to activate the muscles necessary for well-coordinated turnout. The implicit aspect of the imagery would also promote ideal balance between deep stabilisers and global muscles.

The inclusion of creative skills exercises provides each student with autonomy in decision-making and in validating their own ideas. Creative skills training can support their sense of self, building confidence as they face ballet technique's external measures of achievement. Sensory, musical or emotional awareness are aspects of a person's inner experience and are not always responsive to normal instructive techniques, but teachers can inspire their students to awaken and foster these sensibilities within themselves. To assist in the discovery process, teachers can offer subtle, non-intrusive guidance and allow students as much time as they need to develop their own discoveries. Teachers should not expect students to explain their learning because translating sensory and emotional discoveries into verbal form can undermine the implicit nature of their experiences.

Along with previously suggested approaches and exercises for stimulating students' creativity and artistry, imagination should be integral to all dancing, including in class. Some approaches relate closely to technique, creating implicit cues that will increase motor control. The following imagery places the deep abdominal stabilisers at the forefront of the sensorimotor system's planning, even though the quoted dancer uses that imagery simply because it aligns with sensations he has found to be helpful.

> *Recently I've been visualising a steaming, calm lake around my abdomen area through the whole barre. It's a sensation that becomes part of all the movements I do, giving them a groundedness and ease.*

Imagination can also influence the quality and dynamics of movement. Colours and smells are as real to the sensorimotor system as actual sensations of temperature, touch and pain, so they too can influence a movement's dynamics, musicality and expressiveness.

> *Sometimes I get a really strong sensation of a colour. It's as if that colour is part of the movement. Sometimes I deliberately try to zero in on a colour or a smell that corresponds with the movement to inform how I dance it – this one is really zesty and orange, so I can feel that as I dance. But this one is really smoky, earthy and grey.*

Imagination can be a supportive companion for a dancer. Many of us started dancing because we imagined ourselves telling stories and expressing emotions on stage, and we were driven by the sensuality of movement and music. As technical demands increase, these goals can become overwhelmed by the struggle to control our bodies, to gain more turnout, higher extensions and better line, leading some to question whether dance is 'for them'.

> *It's so easy to get in your head and start psyching yourself out or obsessing about one thing. We become so self-critical and obsessed with the refinement of the technique we can lose the sense of why we dance.*

Although few have the physical capacity to perform at the technical level required by professional companies, the deeply joyful experience of participating in ballet classes is not to be underestimated. For all dancers, professional or not, the key to dancing well lies in the imaginative capacity that attracted them to dance in the first place.

> *You ride the music and allow these kinds of inner images and sensations to guide you through the movements.*

While imagination explores the world of thoughts, emotions and ideas, curiosity asks why, how, where, when and why not. Children are naturally curious about the world around them, but this invaluable quality can be buried under the avalanche of information they receive in the name of education. Curiosity, however, leads to new discoveries, expansion of delivered information. An unusual sound in the distance, an unfamiliar word, a newspaper or book, a sculpture or painting, a busker playing an old violin, strange shadows created by irregularly shaped buildings, in fact any sensory, emotional or mental experience can stimulate curiosity. Sometimes, these experiences create immediate knowledge and understanding, but others add themselves to our rich store of 'curiosities', held in our mind until new experiences reveal their meaning. As each new performance challenge arises, our private curiosity store delivers its rich images and concepts to support and extend our artistry.

Learning ballet technique involves an avalanche of information, both physical and mental, and the absolutist nature of technical rules can preclude curiosity about other possibilities. In class, a student is unlikely to follow their curiosity about the required pelvic alignment in *retiré* by experimenting with unconventional alignments during class practice time. Appropriate pelvic alignment is welcome, but anything else is definitely not. But why should a student not broaden their knowledge by exploring options? Depending on how it is taught, ballet technique may either discourage or encourage curiosity. Exploring options will not lead to anarchy. In fact, exploration is essential for progress in any field. Teachers should bear in mind that curiosity enables and encourages dancers to flourish, both technically and creatively.

> *Curiosity gives you hope, because the more you learn about the depth, breadth and complexity of something, the easier it is to find your place within it – and to have the confidence to express yourself uniquely. Keeping your mindset within very strict, tight parameters is damaging to yourself, your own creativity and the art form as a whole, because there's all this depth and richness within that's never tapped.*

Curiosity leads to progress. If William Forsythe had not been curious about what would happen if he displaced a dancer's pelvis and extended shapes beyond technical convention, the 1987 dance world would not have been astounded by *In the Middle, Somewhat Elevated*, and 21st-century choreography may have followed a less interesting path. Like choreographers, dancers develop their performances through their curiosity:

- How might I transform this movement so it is closer to the choreographer's vision?
- Does this character have to be as passive as usually portrayed, or would a more energetic approach help 'flesh out' the drama?
- What would happen if I grounded certain phrases instead of following their usual light and airy dynamic?

Curiosity is also important to dancers as citizens of the world. Although their daily schedule can occupy many of their waking hours, dancers can still read books, follow current affairs and pursue any topic that interests them. Many dancers tour internationally, exposing them to new cultures and knowledge. Dancers are increasingly taking up academic

*Figure 11.2 In the Middle, Somewhat Elevated* by William Forsythe; Ballet Frankfurt, Andrea Megarese, Isabel Gerber.
Source: Photographer: Dominik Mentzos.

studies while they are dancing – a strategy not only offering qualifications for later life, but also expanding their view of the world and making them more interesting people. This expansion of ideas and experiences enriches each dancer's sense of style. Regardless of its brilliance, technique would not hold an audience's attention for long.

A vivid and adaptable sense of style is essential in a professional dancer – a simple movement phrase looks completely different in Petipa's *The Sleeping Beauty* from a similar movement in Forsythe's daringly virtuosic *The Vertiginous Thrill of Exactitude*.

Style is difficult to explain in dance. Style involves a change in the dancer's mindset, which triggers a transformation of the choreography through a multitude of small adaptations according to the choreographer's and dancer's vision. The quality of a head movement; commanding, enticing or subservient shoulders; or an aggressive, playful or arrogant movement style – all these adaptations can reflect the dancer's personality, the situation, and the social and cultural environment of a role. However, style is not necessarily created through conscious movement adaptations. Style involves embodying the character's or the ballet's whole spirit or persona. This is true even in plotless or abstract ballets. Dancers perform Balanchine's *Serenade* with an identifiably Balanchine sense of style, but the same dancers dance entirely differently as they take on the brassy persona Balanchine envisaged for *Stars and Stripes*.

Style embraces a sense of play and imagination, and it is just one of many enjoyable aspects of a professional dancer's work. But professional dancers should not have all the fun! A sense of style can be developed throughout training, bringing imagination and

*Figure 11.3* Matthew Ball as Prince Florimund and Yasmine Naghdi as Aurora in The Royal Ballet's *The Sleeping Beauty*.

*Source*: Photograph: Tristram Kenton/*The Guardian*.

*Figure 11.4 The Vertiginous Thrill of Exactitude.* Choreographer William Forsythe. Dancers Vadim Muntagirov and Marianela Nuñez.

*Source*: ©2017 ROH. Photograph by Bill Cooper.

playfulness to daily classes. My teacher would ask advanced students to research a certain historical period and then explore how that period would affect exercises in daily class. We tried to embody the 18th century when Camargo scandalised Paris by shortening her skirts, drawing attention to our neat ankles and the brilliance of our nimble footwork. Embodying the 19th century world of Degas' dancers in rehearsal and on stage, we might adapt our body language to reflect our social status as desirable objects for hire. By contrast, Anna Pavlova's style of movement may have reflected her role as a universally adored star – elegant, charismatic, enticing or soulful at will. Occasional challenges such as this honed each student's view of ballet as a multifaceted language rather than simply a technique. For those who progressed to professional companies, this viewpoint and associated skills helped them to find the style a choreographer was seeking in early rehearsals – an excellent way to acquire important roles in new ballets!

# 12 Discovering the dancer inside

So far, the emphasis has been on students discovering how to dance well – expressively, musically, creatively and technically. Earlier, I stated my belief that teaching is helping someone discover something, but now the emphasis is on helping someone discover who they are as an individual and as an artist. Contrary to normal practice, the proposed teaching philosophy is best served when the discovery process and artistic exploration have been embedded within the student's training from day one.

> *Art is not about impressing someone else, it's about you discovering what you believe is beautiful and sharing that with others.*

Each student's personal development can be assisted or hampered by their ballet training. Teachers sometimes identify a promising student as soon as they enter the studio – their physique, their movement, and their open curiosity about the new experience can hint at potential, so the teacher is likely to focus on maximising that potential. However, many exceptional dancers do not impress at first. A student who makes slow initial progress may develop rapidly after gaining greater self-belief. Students who appear at first glance to be temperamentally unsuited to dance may simply be overwhelmed by the new experience or suffer from unrelated insecurity. They may be held back by their emotional, social or physical situation outside the studio and so be tense and unwilling to trust the strange environment they find themselves in. For students such as these, losing themselves in artistic exploration can be a lifeline. They can discover their core selves: selves who only need a sense of belonging and support to flourish. For a few students from insecure backgrounds, dancing is their life dream. They know instinctively that they must dance, regardless of seemingly insuperable obstacles. They focus intensely on reaching their goals. While students such as these are eager to learn and highly teachable, they need guidance in allowing their bodies sufficient time for technical consolidation as they pursue their passionate drive to dance.

> *My first ballet class was both a revelation and a confirmation. The exercises themselves, the live piano music and the teacher's demonstration revealed the beauty and harmony I was searching for. That first class confirmed my conviction that this was my world, my destiny.*

As mentioned earlier, some ballet teachers place a priority on providing students with a strong technique, as measured through success or otherwise in examinations and competitions. Some believe that competitions and concerts provide students with opportunities to perform, thereby adding the necessary skills and experience for those wishing to become professional dancers. However, the dancers' words throughout this book show that successful dancers regard expressivity throughout the body as fundamental to ballet; not something to be applied on top of technique or acquired 'on the job'. Therefore, this book argues that expressivity should be deeply ingrained in students' technical training from the earliest stages. It is important to develop the emotional range underpinning expressivity and a vocabulary that allows the expression of emotion, ideas and characters, but it is perhaps more important for students to discover how to express their unique selves, their individual identity, through this vocabulary.

> *My dancing is a combination of all that has come before (from research and open-hearted-ness of previous artists, spaces, ideas) and my individual version/approach/moment.*

When we watch dancers, our Mirror Neuron System allows us to share their physical experience and empathise with their emotional state. The Mirror Neuron System explains why audiences are so intrigued by certain dancers whose movement expresses a vibrant inner life – we recognise them as interesting people, so their dancing captivates us. Conversely, there are dancers who perform extremely well – we may admire their virtuosity, but they themselves are not memorable. What do we want to feel, to empathise with, when we watch a dancer? Will we be satisfied by observing their physical beauty and their strong technique? Or do we want a dancer to express their personal insight into dance?

> *My aim is embodiment. This means, for me, a connection to the artistic parts of myself (as a person, a technician and as a character) and the aims I have/objective I am trying to accomplish. Being present and authentic in my approach and trusting that, even though there are always parts of ourselves we don't like – that in the live moment of performance, with skill and intention, that I am enough and more than that, capable of extraordinary things.*

Teachers often encourage role play in young students' classes: 'Imagine you are a prince/princess wearing a crown and jewels'; 'Pretend you are xxx (a famous dancer)'; and 'Walk on stage as if you are performing at the Royal Opera House'. This sort of role play is fun for children, and it can awaken them to the effect of their imagination on their movement. However, their primary focus is on being someone else, and not being themselves, with the inference that their own self is not enough. By contrast, this book proposes that teachers should help each student 'discover who they are as an individual and as an artist'.

> I'm looking for a sense of self in the art form . . . a sense of who they are as individuals, what kind of choices they make. I'm really looking for individuality.
> David Hallberg, Artistic Director of The Australian Ballet

Most of the 19th-century classical ballets tell a story. Some dancers portray various characters to move the narrative forward, while others perform in groups to enhance the mood of the story. The meanings attached to the story and its characters can be manifold. Taking a traditional performance of *The Sleeping Beauty* as an example, the Vision Scene reveals an unhappy prince who becomes besotted with a vision of the enchanted Aurora. Metaphorically, it could mean that we find happiness by following our dream or that, more prosaically, 'love finds a way'. It could even mean that every young man yearns for happiness with a one-hundred-sixteen-year-old princess. On an individual level, each dancer constructs a meaning for the role they are playing. A nymph in the Vision Scene contributes to the meaning of the whole by helping create a vision of beauty and fulfilment. Later story ballets have more complex narratives and more nuanced characters, but the same general framework applies – meaning exists at various levels, from the universal to the personal.

*In story ballets, at times I could be so invested and immersed in the story that I would use that to drive my movements and express the narrative. But I felt this could sometimes interrupt my connection to my body, and it felt very external. This is why non-narrative ballets were more of an explorative and creative experience for me. Not always of course, but mostly.*

The corps de ballet in the second and fourth acts of *Swan Lake* are symbols rather than individuals, so they should share a consistent and readily identifiable meaning with others in their group. Even in rehearsal in practice clothes, nobody should mistake a swan for a Hungarian princess. Meaning is portrayed through the choreography, but it can be immeasurably enhanced by the dancers' performance. For today's audiences, the dancers' 'schooling' can make a 19th-century ballet's lofty themes and classical story-telling both deeper and more accessible, both universal and personal. Schooling is the result of impeccably consistent training, a strong balletic lineage, and artistic integrity shared by every teacher and every dancer on stage. This harmony produces breath-taking performances of the classics by long-established companies such as the Paris Opera Ballet.

Performing in the corps de ballet is an art in itself. Although it is rarely acknowledged, rehearsals help dancers develop similar breathing patterns in addition to uniformity of details such as timing, spacing, leg height and head angle. Then, to perform as a corps de ballet, each dancer must develop a 'sixth sense' like that of migrating starlings. Swarms of starlings can contain many thousands of individual birds, all gliding through ever-changing patterns across the sky. This seeming miracle is achieved by each bird cooperating with its six or seven neighbours, resulting in a flexible form of coordination throughout the giant swarm. Corps de ballets use similar tactics, with each dancer 'feeling like' the dancers close by. Together, they share the dance's meaning, as well as the sensory experiences it evokes.

*There are moments on stage where you feel the entire ensemble's energy, and this is a fantastic feeling. It feels very human, all these individual people with individual lives and stories have come together to share a feeling. You're all part of this same feedback loop of energy, drawing on each other, it's really invigorating.*

Meaning in more recent and plotless ballets is conveyed in a less literal way, usually through various forms of imagery – visual, sensory, kinaesthetic, subjective or metaphorical. In many cases, the set, lighting and staging are integrated with the dancers' movement – an approach that may be guided by the choreographer's vision or by a unified vision created by an entire creative team. A ballet may end with a lone dancer walking upstage until he is out of sight. Apart from the dancer's intention, the meaning will depend on or be transformed by other factors: a snap blackout, a quick or slow fade to black, a descending curtain, an object moving to hide him, an exit through black drapes, or the dancer flying upwards or dropping through a trapdoor. The relationship between the loss of sound, light and movement will influence meaning – does the music fade out before, after or as he disappears? For dancers in a new ballet, the meaning usually emerges in rehearsal, even though many choreographers prefer not to verbalise their private intention in making the work. Rather, they cast dancers they hope will reveal the desired meaning, thereby enriching the choreographer's own intention. The choreographer's meaning may be beyond words, but the combination of dancers' movement qualities, physiques, musicality and unconscious expressivity can enable the choreographer to create a performance experience that cannot be duplicated in any other art form.

> *In Balanchine's* The Four Temperaments, *I associated words, feelings and colours to the steps and music. This makes (at least for me as the performer, but I hope it also resonates with the audience) a deeper expression of the steps of what is otherwise an abstract ballet. While I am not stuck to experiencing the same visualisations each time, I develop guideposts and textures that I can draw upon, pass on to others or take to other roles. Visualisation helps expand the range of tools I have to work with.*

The cult of perfection is a continuing problem in ballet, and one contrary to a healthy mindset at any age. Numerous researchers, including Nordin-Bates (2019), have revealed the potential psychological harm of perfectionism in dancers. While young people with perfectionistic tendencies seem to be attracted to ballet, all students can be harmed by focusing on the impossible ideal. Despite their awareness of the problem, teachers can struggle to avoid the all-pervasive perfectionism in ballet. If they are to remove perfect, correct, incorrect and wrong from their teaching vocabulary, how can they give accurate, helpful feedback?

Even very young students can be introduced to the concept of variability. Ask a student to make a very simple ballet shape they can perform well, say *bras bas*. Ask the rest of the students whether the shape was 'good', and take a photograph. Ask another student to do the same, then take new photographs of another two students in a 'good' *bras bas*. Show the four photographs to all the students, and ask whether there are any differences between them. No doubt, the arms will be slightly different (possibly rounder or more forward) in each of the four photographs. Remind them that each position is good, even though they are very slightly different. Ask an older student to do a series of *battements tendus*, and explain that each one will be very slightly different from each of the others, even though each one might seem to be an ideal *battement tendu*. Chalk lines or a ruler may help show the differences. For slightly older students, introduce the concept of postural sway. Explain that, even if it is not usually noticeable, humans and other vertebrates are always moving slightly because their balance is always changing. Ask a student to stand 'still' with one shoulder in front of, but not touching, a vertical marker such as a door frame. It will soon become clear that the student's shoulder is moving in tiny increments in every direction as their weight shifts due to postural sway. If these concepts are introduced early in training, any notions of perfection and perfect performance should die a natural death through lack of use.

As teachers should be aiming for a continual growth of each student's knowledge and skill, they should comment on the student's progress rather on the result. Compare a student's *tendu* with their previous *tendus* and with their goal, but not against another student or an impossible ideal of a perfect *tendu*. Productive approaches could include:

- You are managing your turnout much better now. Did you feel as if you lost it at any stage?
- What do you think might help next time?

- Did you notice your body was in a better position in those *pliés*? That's a big improvement. What do you think might help you to turn out both legs at the same time?
- How did your legs feel in the *battements tendus*? I noticed your knees were stretching beautifully the whole time. How did you make your legs seem longer and straighter?
- What do you think might make your arm and leg movements feel more musical? Might your breathing help?
- Did your *port de bras* feel good? I noticed it flowed beautifully and fit with the smooth, dreamy music!

Eventually, students and professional dancers need to welcome postural sway and variability as inescapable aspects of performance, particularly high performance. In scientific terms, optimality, or 'best possible' performance, is not less than perfection; it is the human version of perfection. Certainly, this approach is more personalised and initially more time-consuming, but it reaps enduring rewards. As a teacher, you are treating the student as a partner in the discovery process. Your questions help students develop self-awareness and ownership of their progress – vital steps towards the goal of autonomy.

From a purely technical point of view, classical ballet can be regarded as a rules-based form of dancing. Technical rules abound, some created for aesthetic purposes, some in support of virtuosity and a few to facilitate health and physical safety. Technical requirements change over the decades in accordance with various schools of thought, but abiding by the accepted rules of the day can determine whether a student will progress and possibly achieve a professional career. That said, a few extraordinary dancers have created their own way of meeting the criteria underpinning technical rules rather than the rules themselves. A world-renowned ballerina disguised her severely limited turnout by modifying her alignment – an achievement made possible by her exceptional coordination and kinaesthetic intelligence, supported by knowledgeable and creative teachers. As a rule, though, technical conventions do play a large part in students' progress.

Historically, teaching and learning ballet operated within a strongly hierarchical system. Teachers were absolute masters, while students were usually poor, uneducated and dispensable. Although professional dancers are now highly respected, the hierarchical system persists in many of the world's ballet schools. It is common for students to stand silently in a set position until a teacher enters the studio, then perform a *révérence* and wait until the teacher gives permission for them to move to the barre. Similar rituals occur at the end of class, and each individual student must thank the teacher before leaving the studio. Outside the classroom, students are frequently required to stand aside, perform another *révérence*, and wait silently until a teacher has passed by. These customs were, no doubt, created as an expression of respect for those with exceptional knowledge and experience, but they entrench a power dynamic more in keeping with the 17th or 18th century. Many students must perform these rituals several times every day, possibly for ten years. This continual display of subservience must influence young people's sense of autonomy. In many schools, 'humility', or the humbling of oneself, is held up as the hallmark of excellence, and as an absolute requirement for students. Should adolescents be encouraged to regard humility as the most important character trait for 21st-century adults? Students' confidence and self-belief can also be damaged by a relentless focus on perfection – the impossible goal.

How, then, can teachers engender artistic autonomy in their students, while still preparing them to thrive within the diverse cultures of 21st-century ballet companies? I believe the transition to artistic autonomy must begin early, possibly from the first year or two of classes. Autonomy is defined as the capacity to make an informed, uncoerced decision, or 'the ability to make your own decisions about what to do rather than being influenced by someone else or told what to do' (Collins English Dictionary). However, autonomy must always be seen in context. As an example, autonomy does not give a student or professional dancer the right to ignore valid instructions or to cause disruption or harm in their training or working environment. Autonomy must be balanced with the rights of others, including the rights of the choreographer, other dancers and musicians, and the company's right to present a performance of the highest quality possible. Artistic autonomy is an issue of greater subtlety. Many of the dancers contributing to this book revealed a strong sense of artistic autonomy. Their ability to merge the artistic elements within each ballet with their own capacity to contribute to and enrich performances exemplifies artistic autonomy.

> *The music, emotional storytelling, focus on execution and connection I have with another person on stage are all of great importance to me. They make me feel like there is a real purpose to what I am doing and when those elements combine together, it allows me to go into another realm and become the artist who is creating the image and provoking the feeling I want the audience to feel. . . . I believe that is when a performance can really transcend the viewer.*

So how can a dancer's artistic autonomy best serve the performance and the dancer themselves? Firstly, it can be unwise for a dancer to exploit artistic autonomy immediately after a new idea arises. In most instances, an idea is best explored during rehearsals, so any conflict with other artistic or practical elements can be ironed out. Also, inspiration usually develops with practice – a 'great idea' in one rehearsal may transmogrify in subsequent rehearsals into a subtle and finely honed element of the performance. At the other end of the spectrum, practice may reveal its unsuitability. Chance discoveries in rehearsals can add colour and depth to a role. Many of the most remarkable moments have developed over many years of experimentation, with the dancer using their autonomy like a sculptor's chisel, gradually uncovering the core of the meaning they wish to express.

> *I remember watching two principal women dance Juliet. Both danced the final crypt scene beautifully, but I would run to the wings each night to watch the woman from the second cast, because her silent scream was the most organic, real, guttural thing I'd ever seen in a classical ballet. It was like the earth opened up beneath her and all her pain flowed out – like her bones were screaming. The first cast woman was a dancer screaming onstage, the second cast was Juliet screaming with pain for her lost love.*

Each student and each dancer develops according to their individual nature, their life experiences, their training and their artistic environment. As artists, dancers need a broad awareness of life itself, of books, of current affairs and social history, of different cultures and of the arts in general. Although expertise in any specific area is not necessary, dancers need to expand their minds if they are to be interesting performers. Most choreographers draw on a vast repertoire of experiences and influences in making their work, sometimes unaware of the trigger for their inspiration until they see the work on stage. Dancers who have filled their own storehouses of cultural and artistic awareness can respond to the choreographer's search for the ideal dance language for the particular ballet, thereby enjoying one of the greatest outcomes of artistic autonomy – contributing personally to the development of an artistic creation. Similarly, the richness of a dancer's experiences can help them bring new life to well-known ballets, and sometimes imprint their unique identity on a dance or a role.

> *Before I danced the role of Queen of the Wilis in Giselle, the standard approach was of cold, heartless implacability. I performed the Queen as raging with white-hot fury, burning with venomous hatred towards men, the eternal betrayers.*

Creative skills exercises are an excellent introduction to artistry, while the fact that the students must create their own goals and evaluate their achievement from a purely personal point of view is the beginning of artistic autonomy. Teachers can inspire the development of artistic autonomy by what they do not say, more than by what they do say. It is easy to tell a student that a certain movement or position will be better if they change their eyeline in a certain way. If the student is given time to practise the movement but does not experiment without prompting, the teacher could ask questions such as 'Do your head and eyes feel as if they are part of the movement/position?' or 'What would happen if you changed your head position or your eyeline?' or even better, 'Have you left any part of your body out of the picture you are making?'. It may take longer for the student to arrive at a better result, and the result may not be ideal, but the student will have practised evaluating and modifying the movement – skills which will be increasingly valuable as they progress. Training a dancer is an incremental process. The goal should not be for the student to acquire an ideal movement or position in the short term, but for the student to discover how to create and modify movements and positions to meet their technical and artistic criteria in the future.

In contributing to this book, dancers have allowed us to 'know' them – generously offering us insight into their understanding of dance and dancing, their struggles, their discoveries and, most importantly, the wisdom they have accrued through their years of dancing. None of them regard their present knowledge as fixed – they are all still on their individual journeys of discovery, as befitting for all artists. Curiosity, and a sense of wonder at the depth and potential heights of their chosen art form, leads them to search for still more areas of discovery. Dancers see dancing, and ballet, from the inside. They experience the day-to-day 'workings' of ballet – opportunities overlooked, and creative discoveries lost under the many pressures facing those directing and managing companies. Being younger than those who decide policy, repertoire and the company's image, they also live in a different social and cultural world. At best, they have opportunities to work with the most creative and culturally aware choreographers, repetiteurs and artists of their time, and these influences must expand dancers' mindsets. In the past, ballet's master-servant relationship meant dancers simply presented the director's or choreographer's vision. Today's dancers play an active role in the creation of new ballets and revival of existing repertoire, and they express their individual contributions on stage. Some dancers gain an in-depth understanding of ballet's potential in the near and longer term, and their voices should be heard in broader circles. Global corporations now benefit when their boards listen to the views of younger generations. Older audience members of large ballet companies may initially be startled, possibly discomforted, by anything new, but the world we live in is evolving, so change is essential if ballet is to retain relevance.

> *I have a perception that 'old-school' people in the ballet world tend to view curiosity about how the art form could be more – richer, different, expressive in a different way – as being an insult. But I personally think the opposite. I think to not be curious about an art form and its potential is insulting to the art form.*

Teachers often train students for ten or more years before they are accepted into professional companies. The emerging dancer's first contract is a celebratory occasion marking their new status as a professional and a reward for resilience and determination during the vicissitudes of training. For the teacher, it is also a vindication – proof they can bring a dancer to professional standard. As with any major life milestone, we should share in the student's joy but, in fact, they are suddenly at the very beginning of their new life, with all its adult demands. Teachers can be left with the same doubts as parents when their children leave home. Have I done enough to prepare them for what can be a tough world? Should I have pushed harder to overcome their weaknesses? Will they remember the essentials or become bogged down in unnecessary worries? Are they ready?

Preparing a student's transition into the profession can be compared to releasing orphaned native animals into the wild. As with young native creatures, we must ensure they know how to be independent, to find shelter, to nourish themselves and to avoid predators in their new habitat. We should provide our students with some sort of 'Survival Skills for New Dancers': don't take the best place on the barre regardless of how many prizes you have won; keep out of other dancers' way when they are practising; show respect when anyone seems to need silence; don't leave your belongings lying around; always hang up your costume; accept unwelcome casting decisions without complaint and, most important of all, don't criticise other dancers or staff. We want our former students to survive, but also to flourish in their new surroundings, to embrace the different mindset of those whose primary goal is creative artistry rather than passing an exam or audition. Our students must gain a more holistic understanding of their profession by observing the intensity and breadth of successful dancers' approach to rehearsals, especially within the context of their performance on stage. Most exceptional dancers are enriched by their lives outside ballet but, when they are at work, they focus on merging the dancer inside with the dancer on stage. The following words from one of the contributing dancers are a beautiful description of artistic autonomy:

*A sense that my whole body, mind and spirit are aligned towards my goal (story, steps, intention, outcome) and a sense of destiny. That I am meant to be in that moment performing that thing for those people in that place.*

It is hard to imagine a more life-affirming experience.

# Afterword

> Look at life all around; everything is growing, everything is moving forward. Therefore, I recommend keeping in touch with life and with art.
>
> Agrippina Vaganova, revered Russian ballet teacher (1879–1951)

A few people still identify ballet with its aristocratic past, a few with its grand fairy tales and passionate narratives and a few with ballet as an abstract language of ideas. Ballet is all these things and more. We do not want to lose our heritage but we, like Vaganova, must move forward. We, the dancers, teachers, students and audience members of today, must welcome dance and ballet as a reflection of the diverse internal and external aspects of our lives.

In writing this book, I have continued a life-long quest to create a holistic understanding of dance and ballet, to discover a clear biological, neurological, psychological and philosophical thread between learning ballet and its eventual flowering in the profession. Like many dancers, I remember my early training, words, phrases and gestures shaping how I saw ballet and myself as a dancer. Like many, I also had my own inner truth, my own understanding of the expressive power of my body and mind. Again, these personal certainties and formative experiences were integral to me as a dancer and, later, as a teacher and researcher. The synthesis of the child with all that comes after – decades of learning, performing and life experience – is reflected beautifully in William Butler Yeats' poem *Among School Children*, and epitomised in his famous last line:

*How can we know the dancer from the dance?*

# Glossary of ballet terms

**À la seconde**  To the side
**Adage**  Slow, flowing movements
**Allegro**  Fast, bouncy movements
**Arabesque**  A flowing line through the arms, body and one leg while standing on the other leg
**Ballon**  Jump lightness and bounciness
**Battement**  A leg movement from a closed position (1st, 5th) to an open position and back
**Battement frappé**  A sharp, fast foot movement from a position on the ankle
**Battement tendu**  A *battement* with the working leg moving along the floor
**Bras bas**  A low, curved arm position near the body
**Cabriole**  A jump on one leg, with the jumping leg contacting the raised leg before returning to the floor
**Cambré**  A bend of the body
**Chassé**  A travelling movement along the floor with one foot leading and the other 'chasing' it
**Corps de ballet**  The dancers who usually dance as a group
**De côté**  To the side, sideways
**Demi plié**  A bend of the knees with the heels remaining on the floor
**Demi-pointe**  Standing on the balls and toes of the foot
**Développé**  An unfolding of the working leg after passing through *retiré*
**Double tour**  A jump with two turns mid-air
**Enchaînment**  A combination of steps
**Entrechat**  A jump with the legs opening and crossing in the air
**Extension**  Extending the working leg, usually at or above 90°
**Fifth (5th) position**  Standing with legs turned out and the feet crossed so the small toe of the front foot is close to the heel of the back foot
**First (1st) position**  Standing with the heels together and the toes facing outwards
**Fouetté**  A whipping movement of one leg, sometimes with a turn
**Glissade**  A gliding movement along the floor
**Grand allegro**  Large jumping steps
**Grand pas de deux**  A dance for the principal female and male dancer in a classical ballet
**Grand plié**  A bend of the knees until the heels rise from the floor
**Grand pose**  A position with one leg held high
**Grand rond de jambe en l'air**  A round movement with the working leg raised at or above 90°

**Pas de deux**   A dance for two people
**Petit allegro**   An *enchaînement* of small jumps
**Pirouette**   A turn on one leg
**Plié**   A bend of the knees
**Pointe**   Standing with the weight on the tips of the pointed foot
**Pointe shoes**   Shoes that enable dancers to stand on pointe
**Pointe work**   Dancing on the tips of the toes
**Port de bras**   Arm movements, sometimes coordinated with upper body movements
**Retiré**   Standing on one leg with the other knee held at the side and the toes touching the supporting knee
**Révérence**   A formal bow or curtsey
**Rond de jambe en l'air**   A slightly rounded movement with the working leg
**Spot (spotting)**   Keeping the eyes and head focused on one spot for as long as possible during a turn
**Supporting leg**   The standing leg
**Tendu**   Abbreviation of *battement tendu*
**Turnout**   Rotation of the legs in the hip sockets so the knees and toes face sideways
**Working leg**   Gesture leg, not the supporting leg

# References

American Psychiatric Association (2023). *What are anxiety disorders?* https://www.psychiatry.org/Patients-Families/Anxiety-Disorders/What-are-Anxiety-Disorders?

Anema, H. A., & Dijkerman, H. C. (2013). Motor and kinesthetic imagery. In R. Lacey & S. Lawson (Eds.), *Multisensory imagery*. Springer Science+Business Media. Retrieved July 15, 2022, from https://doi.org/10.1007/978-1-4614-5879-1_6

Arendt, H. (1958). *The human condition*. University of Chicago Press.

Asakawa, K. (2009). Flow experience, culture, and well-being: How do autotelic Japanese college students feel, behave, and think in their daily lives? *Journal of Happiness Studies*, *11*(2), 205–223. https://doi.org/10.1007/s10902-008-9132-3

Atamturk, H., & Dincdolek, B. (2021). Effects of dance education on emotional intelligence related outcomes. *Revista Gênero e Interdisciplinaridade*, *2*(1). https://doi.org/10.51249/gei.v2i01.146

Aviezer, H., Trope, Y., & Todorov, A. (2012). Body cues, not facial expressions, discriminate between intense positive and negative emotions. *Science*, *338*(6111), 1225–1229. https://doi.org/10.1126/science.1224313

Bakker, F. C. (1991). Development of personality in dancers: A longitudinal study. *Personality and Individual Differences*, *12*(7), 671–681. https://doi.org/10.1016/0191-8869(91)90222-w

Bastiaansen, J. A. C. J., Thioux, M., & Keysers, C. (2009). Evidence for mirror systems in emotions. *Philosophical Transactions of the Royal Society B: Biological Sciences*, *364*(1528), 2391–2404. https://doi.org/10.1098/rstb.2009.0058

Bellan, V., Wallwork, S., Gallace, A., Spence, C., & Moseley, G. L. (2017). Integrating self-localization, proprioception, pain, and performance. *Journal of Dance Medicine & Science*, *21*(1), 24–35. https://doi.org/10.12678/1089-313x.21.1.24

Benson, B. L., Anguera, J. A., & Seidler, R. D. (2011). A spatial explicit strategy reduces error but interferes with sensorimotor adaptation. *Journal of Neurophysiology*, *105*(6), 2843–2851. https://doi.org/10.1152/jn.00002.2011

Bernardi, L., Porta, C., & Sleight, P. (2005). Cardiovascular, cerebrovascular, and respiratory changes induced by different types of music in musicians and non-musicians: The importance of silence. *Heart*, *92*(4), 445–452. https://doi.org/10.1136/hrt.2005.064600

Bernardi, N., Bellemare-Pepin, A., & Peretz, I. (2017). Enhancement of pleasure during spontaneous dance. *Frontiers in Human Neuroscience*, *11*. https://doi.org/10.3389/fnhum.2017.00572

Bernstein, N. (1967). *The co-ordination and regulation of movements*. Pergamon Press.

Blasis, C. (1830). *The code of Terpsichore: The art of dancing*. Edward Bull.

Bogodistov, Y., & Dost, F. (2017). Proximity begins with a smile, but which one? Associating non-duchenne smiles with higher psychological distance. *Frontiers in Psychology*, *8*. https://doi.org/10.3389/fpsyg.2017.01374

Burin, A. B., & Osório, F. L. (2017). Music performance anxiety: A critical review of etiological aspects, perceived causes, coping strategies and treatment. *Archives of Clinical Psychiatry (São Paulo)*, *44*(5), 127–133. https://doi.org/10.1590/0101-60830000000136

Burzynska, A. Z., Finc, K., Taylor, B. K., Knecht, A. M., & Kramer, A. F. (2017). The dancing brain: Structural and functional signatures of expert dance training. *Frontiers in Human Neuroscience*, *11*. https://doi.org/10.3389/fnhum.2017.00566

Carattini, C. (2020). *Psychological skills in ballet training: An approach to pedagogy for the fulfilment of student potential* (DCI). Queensland University of Technology.

Carpenter, R., & Noorani, I. (2017). Movement suppression: Brain mechanisms for stopping and stillness. *Philosophical Transactions of the Royal Society B: Biological Sciences*, *372*(1718), 20160542. https://doi.org/10.1098/rstb.2016.0542

Carroll, N., & Moore, M. (2008). Feeling movement: Music and Dance. *Revue internationale de philosophie*, *246*, 413–435. https://doi.org/10.3917/rip.246.0413

Chan, M. Y. (2011). *The relationship between music performance anxiety, age, self-esteem, and performance outcomes in Hong Kong music students* [Durham theses]. Durham University. Available at Durham E-Theses Online: http://etheses.dur.ac.uk/637/

Christensen, J. F., Gaigg, S. B., & Calvo-Merino, B. (2017). I can feel my heartbeat: Dancers have increased interoceptive accuracy. *Psychophysiology*, *55*(4), e13008. https://doi.org/10.1111/psyp.13008

Cirelli, L. K., Einarson, K. M., & Trainor, L. J. (2014). Interpersonal synchrony increases prosocial behavior in infants. *Developmental Science*, *17*(6), 1003–1011. https://doi.org/10.1111/desc.12193

Cottingham, M. D., Johnson, A. H., & Erickson, R. J. (2017). I can never be too comfortable: Race, gender, and emotion at the hospital bedside. *Qualitative Health Research*, *28*(1), 145–158. https://doi.org/10.1177/1049732317737980

Coxon, J. P., Stinear, C. M., & Byblow, W. D. (2007). Selective inhibition of movement. *Journal of Neurophysiology*, *97*(3), 2480–2489. https://doi.org/10.1152/jn.01284.2006

Csíkszentmihályi, M. (1990). *Flow: The psychology of optimal experience*. Harper and Row.

Damasio, A. R. (2000). *The feeling of what happens: Body, emotion and the making of consciousness*. Vintage, Cop.

Damasio, A. R. (2019). *The strange order of things: Life, feeling, and the making of cultures*. Vintage Books.

Damasio, A. R. (2022). *Feeling and knowing: Making minds conscious*. Robinson.

Damasio, A. R., & Carvalho, G. B. (2013). The nature of feelings: Evolutionary and neurobiological origins. *Nature Reviews Neuroscience*, *14*(2), 143–152. https://doi.org/10.1038/nrn3403

Darwin, C. (2018). *The expression of the emotions in man and animals*. Dover Publications, Inc (Original work published 1872).

Davids, K., Button, C., & Bennett, S. (2008). *Dynamics of skill acquisition: A constraints-led approach*. Human Kinetics.

de Manzano, O., Theorell, T., Harmat, L., & Ullén, F. (2010). The psychophysiology of flow during piano playing. *Emotion (Washington, D.C.)*, *10*(3), 301–311. https://doi.org/10.1037/a0018432

Demarin, V., Morovic, S., & Bene, R. (2014). Neuroplasticity. *Periodicum Biologorum*, *116*(2), 209–211. https://doi.org/10.18054

de Melo, C. M., Kenny, P., & Gratch, J. (2010). Real-time expression of affect through respiration. *Computer Animation and Virtual Worlds*, *21*(3–4), 225–234. https://doi.org/10.1002/cav.349

Desai, R. H., Binder, J. R., Conant, L. L., Mano, Q. R., & Seidenberg, M. S. (2011). The neural career of sensory-motor metaphors. *Journal of Cognitive Neuroscience*, *23*(9), 2376–2386. https://doi.org/10.1162/jocn.2010.21596

Dietrich, A. (2004). Neurocognitive mechanisms underlying the experience of flow. *Consciousness and Cognition*, *13*(4), 746–761. https://doi.org/10.1016/j.concog.2004.07.002

Dordevic, M., Schrader, R., Taubert, M., Müller, P., Hökelmann, A., & Müller, N. G. (2018). Vestibulo-hippocampal function is enhanced and brain structure altered in professional ballet dancers. *Frontiers in Integrative Neuroscience*, *12*. https://doi.org/10.3389/fnint.2018.00050

Enea, V., & Iancu, S. (2015). Processing emotional body expressions: State-of-the-art. *Social Neuroscience*, *11*(5), 495–506. https://doi.org/10.1080/17470919.2015.1114020

Faisal, A. A., Selen, L. P. J., & Wolpert, D. M. (2008). Noise in the nervous system. *Nature Reviews Neuroscience*, *9*(4), 292–303. https://doi.org/10.1038/nrn2258

Ferrel-Chapus, C., Hay, L., Olivier, I., Bard, C., & Fleury, M. (2002). Visuomanual coordination in childhood: Adaptation to visual distortion. *Experimental Brain Research*, *144*(4), 506–517. https://doi.org/10.1007/s00221-002-1064-2

Flor, H. (2002). Phantom-limb pain: Characteristics, causes, and treatment. *The Lancet Neurology*, *1*(3), 182–189. https://doi.org/10.1016/s1474-4422(02)00074-1

García-Gómez, M., Guerra, J., López-Ramos, V. M., & Mestre, J. M. (2019). Cognitive fusion mediates the relationship between dispositional mindfulness and negative effects: A study in a sample of Spanish children and adolescent school students. *International Journal of Environmental Research and Public Health*, *16*(23), 4687. https://doi.org/10.3390/ijerph16234687

Gäumann, S., Gerber, R. S., Suica, Z., Wandel, J., & Schuster-Amft, C. (2021). A different point of view: The evaluation of motor imagery perspectives in patients with sensorimotor impairments in a longitudinal study. *BMC Neurology*, *21*(1). https://doi.org/10.1186/s12883-021-02266-w

Gomes, N., Cochet, S., & Guyon, A. (2021). Dance and embodiment: Therapeutic benefits on body-mind health. *Journal of Interdisciplinary Methodologies and Issues in Science, 9*. https://doi.org/10.18713/JIMIS-02072021-9-4.

Grandey, A. A., & Sayre, G. M. (2019). Emotional labor: Regulating emotions for a wage. *Current Directions in Psychological Science*, *28*(2), 131–137. https://doi.org/10.1177/0963721418812771

Gray, R. (2020). Changes in movement coordination associated with skill acquisition in baseball batting: Freezing/freeing degrees of freedom and functional variability. *Frontiers in Psychology, 11*. https://doi.org/10.3389/fpsyg.2020.01295

Green, J. (2002). Somatic knowledge: The body as content and methodology in dance education. *Journal of Dance Education*, *2*(4), 114–118. https://doi.org/10.1080/15290824.2002.10387219

Guimarães, A. N., Ugrinowitsch, H., Dascal, J. B., Porto, A. B., & Okazaki, V. H. A. (2020). Freezing degrees of freedom during motor learning: A systematic review. *Motor Control*, 1–15. https://doi.org/10.1123/mc.2019-0060

Haggard, P. (2005). Conscious intention and motor cognition. *Trends in Cognitive Sciences*, *9*(6), 290–295. https://doi.org/10.1016/j.tics.2005.04.012

Hamill, J., Palmer, C., & Van Emmerik, R. E. A. (2012). Coordinative variability and overuse injury. *Sports Medicine, Arthroscopy, Rehabilitation, Therapy & Technology*, *4*(1). https://doi.org/10.1186/1758-2555-4-45

Hänggi, J., Koeneke, S., Bezzola, L., & Jäncke, L. (2010). Structural neuroplasticity in the sensorimotor network of professional female ballet dancers. *Human Brain Mapping*, *31*(8), 1196–1206. https://doi.org/10.1002/hbm.20928

Hayes-Skelton, S. A., & Eustis, E. H. (2020). Experiential avoidance. In J. S. Abramowitz & S. M. Blakey (Eds.), *Clinical handbook of fear and anxiety: Maintenance processes and treatment mechanisms* (pp. 115–131). American Psychological Association. https://doi.org/10.1037/0000150-007

Immordino-Yang, M. H., & Damasio, A. (2011). We feel, therefore we learn: The relevance of affective and social neuroscience to education. *Learning Landscapes*, *5*(1), 115–131. https://doi.org/10.36510/learnland.v5i1.535

James, W. (1890). *The principles of psychology*. Henry Holt and Company. http://dx.doi.org/10.1037/11059-000

Jaque, S. V., Thomson, P., Zaragoza, J., Werner, F., Podeszwa, J., & Jacobs, K. (2020). Creative flow and physiologic states in dancers during performance. *Frontiers in Psychology, 11*. https://doi.org/10.3389/fpsyg.2020.01000

Jerath, R., & Beveridge, C. (2020). Respiratory rhythm, autonomic modulation, and the spectrum of emotions: The future of emotion recognition and modulation. *Frontiers in Psychology, 11*. https://doi.org/10.3389/fpsyg.2020.01980

Juslin, P. N., & Laukka, P. (2010). Expression, perception, and induction of musical emotions: A review and a questionnaire study of everyday listening. *Journal of New Music Research*, *33*(3), 217–238. https://doi.org/10.1080/0929821042000317813

Karimi, F., Soltani, M., Shaterzadeh Yazdi, M. J., Moradi, N., Shahriari, S., & Latifi, S. M. (2019). The effect of knowledge of result feedback timing on speech motor learning in healthy adults. *Iranian Rehabilitation Journal*, 171–180. https://doi.org/10.32598/irj.17.2.171

Karin, J., Christensen, J., & Haggard, P. (2016). Mental training. In *Dancer wellness*. Human Kinetics.

Kenny, D. T. (2011). Defining music performance anxiety. *The Psychology of Music Performance Anxiety*, 47–82. https://doi.org/10.1093/acprof:oso/9780199586141.003.0027

Khoshnoud, S., Alvarez Igarzábal, F., & Wittmann, M. (2020). Peripheral-physiological and neural correlates of the flow experience while playing video games: A comprehensive review. *PeerJ*, *8*. https://doi.org/10.7717/peerj.10520

Kirschner, S., & Tomasello, M. (2010). Joint music making promotes prosocial behavior in 4-year-old children☆, ☆☆. *Evolution and Human Behavior*, *31*(5), 354–364. https://doi.org/10.1016/j.evolhumbehav.2010.04.004

Kordahi, Y., & Hassmén, P. (2022). Are dancers more emotionally intelligent and self-regulated than non-dancers? *Research in Dance Education*, 1–12. https://doi.org/10.1080/14647893.2022.2097657

Larsen, R. J., Kasimatis, M., & Frey, K. (1992). Facilitating the furrowed brow: An unobtrusive test of the facial feedback hypothesis applied to unpleasant affect. *Cognition and Emotion*, *6*(5), 321–338. https://doi.org/10.1080/02699939208409689

Latash, M. L. (2012). The bliss (not the problem) of motor abundance (not redundancy). *Experimental Brain Research*, *217*(1), 1–5. https://doi.org/10.1007/s00221-012-3000-4

LeDoux, J. (2012). Rethinking the emotional brain. *Neuron*, *73*(5), 1052. https://doi.org/10.1016/j.neuron.2012.02.018

Levin, M. E., MacLane, C., Daflos, S., Seeley, J. R., Hayes, S. C., Biglan, A., & Pistorello, J. (2014). Examining psychological inflexibility as a transdiagnostic process across psychological disorders. *Journal of Contextual Behavioral Science*, *3*(3), 155–163. https://doi.org/10.1016/j.jcbs.2014.06.003

Levitin, D. J., & Tirovolas, A. K. (2009). Current advances in the cognitive neuroscience of music. *Annals of the New York Academy of Sciences*, *1156*, 211–231. https://doi.org/10.1111/j.1749-6632.2009.04417.x

Lewthwaite, R., & Wulf, G. (2010). Social-comparative feedback affects motor skill learning. *Quarterly Journal of Experimental Psychology*, *63*(4), 738–749. https://doi.org/10.1080/17470210903111839

Li, G., He, H., Huang, M., Zhang, X., Lu, J., Lai, Y., Luo, C., & Yao, D. (2015). Identifying enhanced cortico-basal ganglia loops associated with prolonged dance training. *Scientific Reports*, *5*(1). https://doi.org/10.1038/srep10271

Lisberger, S. G., & Medina, J. F. (2015). How and why neural and motor variation are related. *Current Opinion in Neurobiology*, *33*, 110–116. https://doi.org/10.1016/j.conb.2015.03.008

Liu, J., & Wrisberg, C. A. (1997). The effect of knowledge of results delay and the subjective estimation of movement form on the acquisition and retention of a motor skill. *Research Quarterly for Exercise and Sport*, *68*(2), 145–151. https://doi.org/10.1080/02701367.1997.10607990

Lumley, M. A., Cohen, J. L., Borszcz, G. S., Cano, A., Radcliffe, A. M., Porter, L. S., Schubiner, H., & Keefe, F. J. (2011). Pain and emotion: A biopsychosocial review of recent research. *Journal of Clinical Psychology*, *67*(9), 942–968. https://doi.org/10.1002/jclp.20816

Magill, R. A., & Anderson, D. (2014). *Motor learning and control: Concepts and applications*. 10th edition. McGraw-Hill Education

Maguire, E. A., Gadian, D. G., Johnsrude, I. S., Good, C. D., Ashburner, J., Frackowiak, R. S. J., & Frith, C. D. (2000). Navigation-related structural change in the hippocampi of taxi drivers. *Proceedings of the National Academy of Sciences*, *97*(8), 4398–4403. https://doi.org/10.1073/pnas.070039597

Marchant, D. C., & Greig, M. (2017). Attentional focusing instructions influence quadriceps activity characteristics but not force production during isokinetic knee extensions. *Human Movement Science*, *52*, 67–73. https://doi.org/10.1016/j.humov.2017.01.007

Margolis, J. (1981). The autographic nature of the dance. *The Journal of Aesthetics and Art Criticism*, *39*(4), 419. https://doi.org/10.2307/430241

Mason, P. (2022). *Understanding the brain: The neurobiology of everyday life*. Presentation.

Masters, R. S. W., & Maxwell, J. (2008). The theory of reinvestment. *International Review of Sport and Exercise Psychology*, *1*(2), 160–183. https://doi.org/10.1080/17509840802287218

Masters, R. S. W., Poolton, J. M., Maxwell, J. P., & Raab, M. (2008). Implicit motor learning and complex decision making in time-constrained environments. *Journal of Motor Behavior*, *40*(1), 71–79. https://doi.org/10.3200/jmbr.40.1.71-80.

Masterson, J. (2015). The role of emotion, vision and touch in movement learning neuroplasticity and the mirror neuron system. *Journal of Psychology & Clinical Psychiatry*, *3*(5). https://doi.org/10.15406/jpcpy.2015.03.00149

Matsumoto, D. (1987). The role of facial response in the experience of emotion: More methodological problems and a meta-analysis. *Journal of Personality and Social Psychology*, *52*(4), 769–774. https://doi.org/10.1037/0022-3514.52.4.769

Mehling, W. E., Gopisetty, V., Daubenmier, J., Price, C. J., Hecht, F. M., & Stewart, A. (2009). Body awareness: Construct and self-report measures. *PLoS ONE*, *4*(5), e5614. https://doi.org/10.1371/journal.pone.0005614

Merchant, H., Grahn, J., Trainor, L., Rohrmeier, M., & Fitch, W. T. (2015). Finding the beat: A neural perspective across humans and non-human primates. *Philosophical Transactions of the Royal Society B: Biological Sciences*, *370*(1664), 20140093. https://doi.org/10.1098/rstb.2014.0093

Moors, A., & Fischer, M. (2018). Demystifying the role of emotion in behaviour: Toward a goal-directed account. *Cognition and Emotion*, *33*(1), 94–100. https://doi.org/10.1080/02699931.2018.1510381

Moseley, G. L. (2003). A pain neuromatrix approach to patients with chronic pain. *Manual Therapy*, *8*(3), 130–140. https://doi.org/10.1016/s1356-689x(03)00051-1

Moseley, L. G., & Arntz, A. (2007). The context of a noxious stimulus affects the pain it evokes. *Pain*, *133*(1), 64–71. https://doi.org/10.1016/j.pain.2007.03.002

Nigmatullina, Y., Hellyer, P. J., Nachev, P., Sharp, D. J., & Seemungal, B. M. (2013). The neuroanatomical correlates of training-related perceptuo-reflex uncoupling in dancers. *Cerebral Cortex*, *25*(2), 554–562. https://doi.org/10.1093/cercor/bht266

Noguchi, K., Masaoka, Y., Satoh, K., Katao, N., & Homma, I. (2012). Effect of music on emotions and respiration. *The Showa University Journal of Medical Sciences*, *24*(1), 69–75. https://doi.org/10.15369/sujms.24.69

Noh, Y. E., Morris, T., & Andersen, M. B. (2003). Psychosocial stress and injury in dance. *Journal of Physical Education, Recreation & Dance*, *74*(4), 36–40. https://doi.org/10.1080/07303084.2003.10609200

Nordin, A. D., & Dufek, J. S. (2019). Reviewing the variability-overuse injury hypothesis: Does movement variability relate to landing injuries? *Research Quarterly for Exercise and Sport*, *90*(2), 190–205. https://doi.org/10.1080/02701367.2019.1576837

Nordin-Bates, S. M. (2019). Striving for perfection or for creativity? *Journal of Dance Education*, *20*(1), 23–34. https://doi.org/10.1080/15290824.2018.1546050

Nummenmaa, L., Glerean, E., Hari, R., & Hietanen, J. K. (2013). Bodily maps of emotions. *Proceedings of the National Academy of Sciences*, *111*(2), 646–651. https://doi.org/10.1073/pnas.1321664111

Nuyens, F. M., Kuss, D. J., Lopez-Fernandez, O., & Griffiths, M. D. (2019). The potential interaction between time perception and gaming: A narrative review. *International Journal of Mental Health and Addiction*, *18*, 1226–1246. https://doi.org/10.1007/s11469-019-00121-1

Orth, D., van der Kamp, J., Memmert, D., & Savelsbergh, G. J. P. (2017). Creative motor actions as emerging from movement variability. *Frontiers in Psychology*, *8*. https://doi.org/10.3389/fpsyg.2017.01903

Ostry, D. J., Darainy, M., Mattar, A. A. G., Wong, J., & Gribble, P. L. (2010). Somatosensory plasticity and motor learning. *Journal of Neuroscience*, *30*(15), 5384–5393. https://doi.org/10.1523/jneurosci.4571-09.2010

Otte, F. W., Davids, K., Millar, S.-K., & Klatt, S. (2020). When and how to provide feedback and instructions to athletes? How sport psychology and pedagogy insights can improve coaching interventions to enhance self-regulation in training. *Frontiers in Psychology, 11.* https://doi.org/10.3389/fpsyg.2020.01444

Phillips-Silver, J., & Trainor, L. J. (2005). Feeling the beat: Movement influences infant rhythm perception. *Science, 308*(5727), 1430–1430. https://doi.org/10.1126/science.1110922

Poolton, J. M., & Zachry, T. L. (2007). So you want to learn implicitly? Coaching and learning through implicit motor learning techniques. *International Journal of Sports Science & Coaching, 2*(1), 67–78. https://doi.org/10.1260/174795407780367177

Ramachandran, V. S., & Altschuler, E. L. (2009). The use of visual feedback, in particular mirror visual feedback, in restoring brain function. *Brain, 132*(7), 1693–1710. https://doi.org/10.1093/brain/awp135

Rizzolatti, G., & Craighero, L. (2004). The mirror-neuron system. *Annual Review of Neuroscience, 27*(1), 169–192. https://doi.org/10.1146/annurev.neuro.27.070203.144230

Rizzolatti, G., & Sinigaglia, C. (2010). The functional role of the parieto-frontal mirror circuit: Interpretations and misinterpretations. *Nature Reviews Neuroscience, 11*(4), 264–274. https://doi.org/10.1038/nrn2805

Royce, A. R. (2002). *The anthropology of dance.* Dance Books.

Runco, M. A., & Jaeger, G. J. (2012). The standard definition of creativity. *Creativity Research Journal, 24*(1), 92–96. https://doi.org/10.1080/10400419.2012.650092

Sakaguchi, Y., & Aiba, E. (2016). Relationship between musical characteristics and temporal breathing pattern in piano performance. *Frontiers in Human Neuroscience, 10,* 381. https://doi.org/10.3389/fnhum.2016.00381

Santanello, A. W., & Gardner, F. L. (2006). The role of experiential avoidance in the relationship between maladaptive perfectionism and worry. *Cognitive Therapy and Research, 31*(3), 319–332. https://doi.org/10.1007/s10608-006-9000-6

Sawyer, K. (2011). The cognitive neuroscience of creativity: A critical review. *Creativity Research Journal, 23*(2), 137–154. https://doi.org/10.1080/10400419.2011.571191

Serrano, T., & Espirito-Santo, H. A. (2017). Music, ballet, mindfulness, and psychological inflexibility. *Psychology of Music, 45*(5), 725–738. https://doi.org/10.1177/0305735616689298

Sharma, D. A., Chevidikunnan, M. F., Khan, F. R., & Gaowgzeh, R. A. (2016). Effectiveness of knowledge of result and knowledge of performance in the learning of a skilled motor activity by healthy young adults. *Journal of Physical Therapy Science, 28*(5), 1482–1486. https://doi.org/10.1589/jpts.28.1482

Smith, A. M., & Messier, C. (2014). Voluntary out-of-body experience: An fMRI study. *Frontiers in Human Neuroscience, 8.* https://doi.org/10.3389/fnhum.2014.00070

Solodkin, A., Hlustik, P., Chen, E. E., & Small, S. L. (2004). Fine modulation in network activation during motor execution and motor imagery. *Cerebral Cortex, 14*(11), 1246–1255. https://doi.org/10.1093/cercor/bhh086

Stanton, T. R., Moseley, G. L., Wong, A. Y. L., & Kawchuk, G. N. (2017). Feeling stiffness in the back: A protective perceptual inference in chronic back pain. *Scientific Reports, 7.* https://doi.org/10.1038/s41598-017-09429-1

Stein, M. I. (1953). Creativity and culture. *The Journal of Psychology, 36*(2), 311–322. https://doi.org/10.1080/00223980.1953.9712897

Strack, F., Martin, L. L., & Stepper, S. (1988). Inhibiting and facilitating conditions of the human smile: A nonobtrusive test of the facial feedback hypothesis. *Journal of Personality and Social Psychology, 54*(5), 768–777. https://doi.org/10.1037/0022-3514.54.5.768

Sullivan, K. J., Kantak, S. S., & Burtner, P. A. (2008). Motor learning in children: Feedback effects on skill acquisition. *Physical Therapy, 88*(6), 720–732. https://doi.org/10.2522/ptj.20070196

Swinnen, S. P., Schmidt, R. A., Nicholson, D. E., & Shapiro, D. C. (1990). Information feedback for skill acquisition: Instantaneous knowledge of results degrades learning. *Journal of Experimental Psychology: Learning, Memory, and Cognition, 16*(4), 706–716. https://doi.org/10.1037/0278-7393.16.4.706

Tajadura-Jiménez, A., & Tsakiris, M. (2014). Balancing the "inner" and the "outer" self: Interoceptive sensitivity modulates self – other boundaries. *Journal of Experimental Psychology: General*, *143*(2), 736–744. https://doi.org/10.1037/a0033171

Todorov, E., & Jordan, M. I. (2002). Optimal feedback control as a theory of motor coordination. *Nature Neuroscience*, *5*(11), 1226–1235. https://doi.org/10.1038/nn963

van Leeuwen, T. M., Singer, W., & Nikolić, D. (2015). The merit of synesthesia for consciousness research. *Frontiers in Psychology*, *6*. https://doi.org/10.3389/fpsyg.2015.01850

Walker, I. J., & Nordin-Bates, S. M. (2010). Performance anxiety experiences of professional ballet dancers: The importance of control. *Journal of Dance Medicine & Science: Official Publication of the International Association for Dance Medicine & Science*, *14*(4), 133–145

Warr, M., Henriksen, D., & Mishra, P. (2018). Creativity and flow in surgery, music, and cooking: An interview with neuroscientist Charles Limb. *TechTrends*, *62*(2), 137–142. https://doi.org/10.1007/s11528-018-0251-3

Wenger, E., Brozzoli, C., Lindenberger, U., & Lövdén, M. (2017). Expansion and renormalization of human brain structure during skill acquisition. *Trends in Cognitive Sciences*, *21*(12), 930–939. https://doi.org/10.1016/j.tics.2017.09.008

Williams, J. H. G., Huggins, C. F., Zupan, B., Willis, M., Van Rheenen, T. E., Sato, W., Palermo, R., Ortner, C., Krippl, M., Kret, M., Dickson, J. M., Li, C. R., & Lowe, L. (2020). A sensorimotor control framework for understanding emotional communication and regulation. *Neuroscience & Biobehavioral Reviews*, *112*, 503–518. https://doi.org/10.1016/j.neubiorev.2020.02.014

Winckelmann, J. J. (1972). *Writings on art*. London Phaidon Press/New York Phaidon Publishers/New York Praeger Publishers.

Wolfe, S. B. (2006). *Cravings for crime: Addiction to criminal behaviour* [Unpublished master's thesis]. Athabasca University, Alberta, Canada.

Wulf, G., Lauterbach, B., & Toole, T. (1999). The learning advantages of an external focus of attention in golf. *Research Quarterly for Exercise and Sport*, *70*(2), 120–126. https://doi.org/10.1080/02701367.1999.10608029

Wulf, G., & Prinz, W. (2001). Directing attention to movement effects enhances learning: A review. *Psychonomic Bulletin & Review*, *8*(4), 648–660. https://doi.org/10.3758/bf03196201

Yu, Q.-H., Fu, A. S. N., Kho, A., Li, J., Sun, X.-H., & Chan, C. C. H. (2016). Imagery perspective among young athletes: Differentiation between external and internal visual imagery. *Journal of Sport and Health Science*, *5*(2), 211–218. https://doi.org/10.1016/j.jshs.2014.12.008

Zatorre, R. J., Chen, J. L., & Penhune, V. B. (2007). When the brain plays music: Auditory – motor interactions in music perception and production. *Nature Reviews Neuroscience*, *8*(7), 547–558. https://doi.org/10.1038/nrn2152

Zatorre, R. J., Fields, R. D., & Johansen-Berg, H. (2012). Plasticity in gray and white: Neuroimaging changes in brain structure during learning. *Nature Neuroscience*, *15*(4), 528–536. https://doi.org/10.1038/nn.3045

Zatsiorsky, V. M., & Prilutsky, B. I. (2012). *Biomechanics of skeletal muscles*. Human Kinetics.

Zeman, A., Milton, F., Della Sala, S., Dewar, M., Frayling, T., Gaddum, J., Hattersley, A., Heuerman-Williamson, B., Jones, K., MacKisack, M., & Winlove, C. (2020). Phantasia – The psychological significance of lifelong visual imagery vividness extremes. *Cortex*, *130*, 426–440. https://doi.org/10.1016/j.cortex.2020.04.003

# Index

Action Observation Network 60
agonist 54, 68, 78
antagonist 54, 68, 78
anticipatory postural adjustment (APA) 56, 57
anxiety 1, 6, 8, 10, 11, 13, 41, 42, 43, 44, 45, 46, 47, 65
autotelia 7, 8

Balanchine, George 17, 71, 103, 109
Bernstein, Nikolai 36, 51, 54, 55, 56, 72
blacksmith study 51, 54
Blasis, Carlo 30, 33, 35, 71, 90
Bournonville, August 31, 33
*The Burrow* 35

central nervous system (CNS) 52, 54, 58, 92
centre of mass (COM) 56, 57
centre of pressure (COP) 57
*The Code of Terpsichore* 30, 33, 90
cognition 9, 37, 62, 100
cognitive fusion 39, 40

declarative knowledge 66, 67
deep (stabilising) muscles 57, 58
degrees of freedom 52, 54, 55, 56, 68, 77, 86, 87
Duchenne smile 14, 91
Duncan, Isadora 34

embodiment 11, 33, 51, 107
endocrine (hormone) system 52
errorless learning 66
experiential avoidance 39, 40
explicit learning 42, 66, 67, 90
extra-corporeal experience 9

feedback 7, 12, 14, 17, 42, 47, 48, 53, 57, 58, 59, 60, 77, 78, 79, 80, 81, 82, 83, 91, 92, 108, 109
feed-forward 58
flow 1, 6, 8, 9, 10, 13, 16, 20, 24, 37, 52, 63, 64, 66, 71, 87, 88, 89, 91, 95, 96, 110, 111, 114, 115

focus of attention (FOA) 67, 68
Fokine, Michel 71
Forsythe, William 89, 102, 103, 104
functional plasticity 37
*The Four Temperaments* 109

global muscles 57, 101
Graham, Martha 34, 35, 99
gray matter (brain) 37, 55, 56

Hallberg, David 107
hyper-vigilance 45

imagery 13, 20, 22, 24, 42, 58, 59, 62, 63, 64, 65, 66, 68, 75, 77, 78, 80, 86, 87, 88, 89, 90, 95, 98, 100, 101, 108
implicit learning 42, 56, 66, 67, 68, 79, 90, 100
*In the Middle, Somewhat Elevated* 102, 103

kinaesthesia 53
kinaesthetic 18, 42, 63, 64, 79, 87, 88, 98, 108, 110,
kinematics 64
kinetic 64
King Louis XlV 24, 3090
Knowledge of Performance (KP) 80, 81
Knowledge of Results (KR) 80
KR-delay interval 81

*La Bayadère* 21, 22, 72
*La Sylphide* 33, 71
*Les Sylphides* 71
*The Lilac Garden* 35
long-term memory 66

MacMillan, Kenneth 35
McGregor, Wayne 23, 89
mental practice 65
mental rehearsal 65
mental representation 66
metaphor 13, 42, 64, 65, 66, 68, 87, 107, 108
Mirror Neuron System 38, 59, 60, 61, 72, 77, 91, 107

motor control 16, 23, 36, 38, 52, 53, 54, 55, 59, 65, 77, 78, 80, 84, 86, 88, 91, 92, 99, 101
motor cortex 53, 54, 78
motor learning 38, 55, 58, 61, 62, 66, 67, 79, 81, 92
motor system 2, 12, 16, 22, 23, 49, 51, 52, 53, 54, 55, 56, 57, 58, 60, 62, 63, 64, 66, 67, 68, 77, 78, 79, 81, 82, 83, 86, 87, 88, 89, 90, 92, 93, 97, 98, 100, 101
movement inhibition 54
movement suppression 54

*Napoli* 33
neural feedback 58
neural variability 54
neuroplasticity 61
non-selective inhibition 54

out-of-body experience 9

pain 1, 18, 30, 41, 44, 45, 46, 47, 63, 64, 97, 101, 111
Paris Opera Ballet 60, 108
Paris Opera Ballet School 30
perfectionism 39, 41, 109
peripheral nervous system (PNS) 52
Petipa, Marius 33, 71, 72, 103
phantasia 65, 66
plasticity 37, 38, 54, 61
post-KR interval 81
postural sway 36, 56, 57, 59, 109, 110
predictive model 53
pronate 55
proprioception 53
psychological inflexibility 39, 40
psychological skills 40, 46, 71, 75, 91

Raymonda 28
reinvestment 67

selective inhibition 54
self-esteem 8, 43, 65, 91
sensorimotor system 12, 22, 52, 58, 62, 63, 78, 79, 82, 83, 87, 88, 91, 92, 97, 98, 101
sensory feedback 12, 42, 47, 53, 58, 78, 82, 83
*The Sleeping Beauty* 33, 103, 104, 107
social anxiety 42
somatic 22, 41, 45, 52, 53, 58, 59, 62, 79
spatial working memory 38
stabilising muscles 57, 67
structural plasticity 37, 38
subjective awareness 12
superficial (global) muscles 44, 57
supinate 55
*Swan Lake* 24, 26, 33, 71, 108

Tchaikovsky, Pyotr Ilyich 33
trait anxiety 8
trauma 43, 44
trial and error 66, 90
Tudor, Antony 35

Vaganova, Agrippina 71, 114
variability 10, 12, 23, 36, 52, 54, 55, 56, 88, 91, 109, 110
*The Vertiginous Thrill of Exactitude* 103, 104
vestibular system 38, 53, 59
visualisation 62, 109
voluntary extra-corporeal experience 9

white matter (brain) 38
working memory 38, 42, 66, 67

# Taylor & Francis eBooks

www.taylorfrancis.com

A single destination for eBooks from Taylor & Francis with increased functionality and an improved user experience to meet the needs of our customers.

90,000+ eBooks of award-winning academic content in Humanities, Social Science, Science, Technology, Engineering, and Medical written by a global network of editors and authors.

TAYLOR & FRANCIS EBOOKS OFFERS:

A streamlined experience for our library customers

A single point of discovery for all of our eBook content

Improved search and discovery of content at both book and chapter level

## REQUEST A FREE TRIAL
support@taylorfrancis.com

For Product Safety Concerns and Information please contact our EU
representative GPSR@taylorandfrancis.com
Taylor & Francis Verlag GmbH, Kaufingerstraße 24, 80331 München, Germany

www.ingramcontent.com/pod-product-compliance
Lightning Source LLC
Chambersburg PA
CBHW060304010526
44108CB00042B/2666